The Laurie Taylor
Guide to Higher Education

The Laurie Taylor
Guide to Higher Education

Laurie Taylor

Illustrated by Sarah Ward

BUTTERWORTH
HEINEMANN

Butterworth-Heinemann
Linacre House, Jordan Hill, Oxford OX2 8DP
A division of Reed Educational and Professional Publishing Ltd

 A member of the Reed Elsevier plc group

OXFORD   BOSTON   JOHANNESBURG
MELBOURNE   NEW DELHI   SINGAPORE

First published 1994
Reprinted 1995, 1996

British Library Cataloguing in Publication Data
Taylor, Laurie
    The Laurie Taylor Guide to Higher Education
    I. Title
    378.41

ISBN 0 7506 2143 5

Printed in Great Britain by Clays Ltd, St Ives plc

Contents

Acknowledgements

I would like to thank Helen Priday of the Times Supplements and Jonathan Glasspool of Butterworth-Heinemann for all their enthusiasm and encouragement; my former colleague at York, Andy Tudor, and my son Matthew, for all their ideas; Cathie Mahoney for her regular laughter; Liz Abi-Aad for her wonderfully good-humoured and very efficient research; Sarah Ward for capturing so much of university life in her drawings; Ralph Steadman for the persistently anarchic influence of his portrait; and the scores of academics who have sent me, often under plain cover, photocopied proof of the diverse forms of madness which have swept over our institutions of higher education since I began these columns just sixteen years ago. I hardly need to add that all the characters described in this book only exist within the fictitious boundaries of the University of Poppleton.

1 The 'new' professors I

Senior academic resigns in protest over wholesale awarding of professorships to those who have not earned them – THES

ARE YOU A PROPER PROFESSOR? BANISH THOSE UGLY DOUBTS AND RECURRENT ANXIETIES BY COMPLETING THIS QUESTIONNAIRE

1 To which of the following aspects of your academic career would you attribute your present title of 'professor'?

a Many years of highly distinguished research

b More years of mediocre research than most of your colleagues

c A majority vote taken at a meeting dominated by people who also fancied themselves as 'professors'

2 Which of the following people routinely refer to you as 'professor' in the course of conversation?

a Your current Vice Chancelor

b Other professors

c Your mother

3 In which of the following places might one currently find a reference to your chair?

a Only on your departmental headed paper

b In your local telephone directory entry

c On your car registration plate

4 Are you a professor in a university which has traditionally contained any of the following features?

a A Senior Common Room

b A Student Refectory

c A Hot Dog Stand

5 Which of the following committee minutes might best characterise your own entry to a meeting?

a The meeting welcomed Professor Dingbat

b The meeting welcomed 'Professor' Dingbat

c The meeting welcomed (Professor) Dingbat

6 Which of the following responses would you most expect to have been uttered by former colleagues on learning of you elevation to a chair?

a 'Quite honestly, it should have happened years ago'

b 'On balance, it's no more than he/she deserves'

c 'Who did you say? Really? Are you sure? A "Professor"? You *must* be joking! Not the one who spoke at last year's Annual Conference? Oh, my God! Whoever next? Talk about a sow's ear. Are you *absolutely* sure?

PROFESSOR CHECK

Score 10 points for all 'a' answers, 5 for all 'b' answers, and 0 for all 'c' answers.

45-60 points. No doubt about it, you're a professor. Well done!

30-45 points. You can certainly call yourself a professor (but to a professor are you a professor?)

0-30 points. You're more of a 'professor' than a professor. Don't worry though. It never did Jimmy Edwards any harm.

1

2 Semesterisation

YOUR QUESTIONS ANSWERED

This week: *Semesterisation*

What is meant by 'semesterisation'?

'Semesterisation' is the breaking up of university courses into two halves of six months each. It's from the Latin *semestris – sex*, six, *mensis*, a month.

So a 'semester' is six months long?

Not necessarily. Leading educational thinkers are currently proposing that each university semester should be 15 weeks long.

So there might be two 15-week semesters in every university year?

There might be. But other leading educational thinkers prefer to talk of semesterisation not as two terms of 15 weeks each year, but as *three* terms of 15 weeks each year.

Supposing we had two 15-week semesters, when would the first one start?

The first semester could start at the beginning of September and finish before Christmas. Or it could start in November and have a midterm break at Christmas. Or it could start in January so everyone would have lots of time to get ready for it. Or it could start in October as it does now.

Then what would happen at Christmas?

Lord Flowers would abolish it.

Why is 'semesterisation' suddenly so important?

Now we've all adopted 'modularisation', there are lots of committees around with no major '-ation' to discuss.

So what are the arguments for a change to the present system?

Experts insist that the present system of three terms is not sufficiently flexible to take account of the changing nature of students entering HE, the proper recognition of CATS (Credit Accumulation and Transfer), and the appropriate knowledge of Prior Experimental Learning (PEL).

Is that the real reason?

Not at all. The Government is totally fed up with students and lecturers having huge long holidays and sees it as a wonderful way of packing in a third more students for little extra cost and setting the stage for the introduction in the near future of 'accelerated degrees' based on two-year courses of 45 weeks a year.

Aren't you being a trifle paranoid?

Where have you been for the past 14 years?

3 Campus universities

A survey of student choices by The Sunday Correspondent reveals a dramatic swing back to the 'green field' campus universities.

Do take a seat. And let me start the proceedings by introducing my colleague, Dr Ritblat.

Good afternoon, Ms Wagstaff.

Good afternoon, Doctor.

Now, Ms Wagstaff, or would you prefer, Charlotte?

Charlotte, please.

Excellent. Now, Charlotte. What exactly is it which particularly attracts you to this university? No need to be nervous. No one here is going to bite.

It's ... it's mostly the ducks.

Very good. That's a useful start, Charlotte, but I'll have to press you a little on that answer. What sort of ducks are we talking about?

I think that it's principally the tufted ducks. The ones near the physics block.

What's so special about the tufted ducks?

It's ... how can I put this, it's ... yes ... it's something to do with their white front and their purpley black tuft.

Yes, I see that. But are we therefore to assume that you have something against all those teals and widgeons down near the admin. building?

No, I've nothing exactly 'against' them. They're very colourful, what with the red and green striped heads of the teals and the goldenish heads of the widgeons, but quite frankly ...

Yes?

Well, I have to say that on the whole I prefer shelduck to both the teal and widgeon. Something about that chestnut plumage when it's set against the concrete of the chemistry complex.

Interesting, Charlotte. Very interesting. But presumably you take the traditional line on our geese. More or less pro-Barnacle but critical of the Canada?

I wouldn't like to be too definitive. Not until I've been here long enough to learn about your culling policies.

A good answer.

Thank you.

Well, I can see that Dr Ritblat is nodding enthusiastically so I don't really think we need to take up any more of your time this afternoon. I'm delighted to be able to offer you a place at this university on condition that you obtain two 'Bs' or their equivalent in your A levels.

Thank you very much.

I must admit I was a shade disappointed to find no mention of our coot or Mandarin Duck in your answers, but I felt you stood your ground extremely well over the general issue of shelduck.

Thank you.

Now, what is the exact combination of subjects you wish to pursue within this faculty?

I'd like to do the joint degree in engineering and metallurgy.

Excellent. Well, we both look forward to seeing you – and, of course, your wellington boots – next October.

3

4 The triumph of theory

Theorists are still in triumphalist mode, cocky, bandwagoning along, a surging band, confident in job security and intellectual prestige – THES

Get to the staff-graduate seminar last night?

Oh yeah. Very tasty.

Really?

We had this bleeder from some old and ancient university talking about what he called 'the incidence of poverty in North-East England'.

Not another toss-pot empiricist?

Right down to the charts and correlations.

So you let him have some?

Oh yeah. Soon as it was question time, up jumps Big Stan and asks how he managed to speak for a whole hour about power in the postmodern world without one mention of Foucault.

Nice one

And when he said he couldn't see what Foucault had to do with the 'basic facts of poverty', Knuckles Paul comes straight in with 'what precisely do you mean by "basic"? How "basic" is "basic"? Is it more "basic" than "fundamental"'?

Gave him a real going over then?

Not half. He started blustering about 'basic' having something to do with minimal nutritional standards as laid down by some agency or other. But absolutely no critical analysis.

Essential crap.

Basically. And so bang on cue up gets Mad Ralph and smacks him round the head with a Derridean metaphysics of presence.

Ooh - Aah - Derri - Dah!

Right on. And then while he's still picking himself up from that one, Razor Kathy nips in sharpish with her usual trope on Kristevan heterogeneity.

And it's all over bar the shouting?

Oh yeah. A vote of thanks from the chairperson. Brief round of applause. And then our lot all go down the boozer for some brand name lager and a few ironic choruses of 'Ere We Go.

Typical sort of academic evening then?

You could say that.

5 Degree day I

TO ALL GRADUANDS
RULES OF PROCEDURE
FOR DEGREE DAY

■ Please make certain that you process to the platform in strict alphabetical order. So, for example, McGreechan always comes before McGreeghan, which in turn, invariably precedes McGreevey.

■ All last-minute absences must be immediately reported to the Convener of Degree Day (Wing Commander D. W. D. Digby). Failure for absences to be noted in the degree lists can result in the unfortunate 'shunting effect' which last year meant 47 graduands were, as they processed across the platform, incorrectly named, and in fourteen cases, erroneously gendered.

■ Geography graduands are reminded that Professor Collingworth is now in his seventy-third year and therefore not able to sustain a prolonged period of hand-shaking. You are therefore requested to mime this part of the proceedings by placing your hand slightly to the right of his and moving it up and down twice in quick succession.

■ Graduands may be photographed with a professor of their choice for the standard fee of £5 per photograph (all proceeds to departmental funds). This offer does not, however, apply this year to Professor Dibson of the anthropology department, who is currently of the opinion that repeated exposure to photography has partially robbed him of his identity.

■ This year's honorary graduates are Mr J. T. R. Property Developer and Mr P. B. W. Industrial Effluent. Both men are friends of the university and should be rapturously received both before and after their receipt of the honorary degree. During their lengthy acceptance speeches, laughter should only occur when the presence of a joke is signalled by the thumbs-up from the deputy bursar (positioned on the right at the rear of the platform).

- We have been advised by Dr S. Q. Lumière of the Audio-Visual Unit (the executive producer in charge of this year's degree video) that a higher quality of production will be obtained if the following instructions are at all times observed.

a   All graduands should ensure that their right foot is on 'the chalk mark' when accepting their degrees.

b   A light foundation make-up should be worn at all times.

c   On no account must the graduands wave in the general direction of the camera when accepting their degree certificates.

- Following a number of representations from individual students, we have decided this year to introduce a special marquee exclusively for those parents who are thought to be 'potentially embarrassing'. Parents who are escorted to this area by their children will not be released until the end of the proceedings.

- We are advised by the Vice Chancellor that, as usual on degree day, he wishes to walk informally among parents and graduates after the ceremony. To avoid a repetition of the unfortunate encounters last year when the Vice Chancellor was not recognised by some of those he approached (and indeed on one occasion was the subject of a minor physical assault) we now advise you that he is approximately 5ft 10in tall, with thinning hair, sallow complexion, and a deep scar running down his right cheek.

Have a nice day.

APPOINTMENTS UNIVERSITY OF POPPLETON

6 The university library I

Alarming erosion of standards in university library provision – report in THES

Madam Chairman, before we turn to departmental allocations I wonder if we might minute my change of title?

I gather we're now to call you 'Chief Librarian' rather than 'Head Librarian'.

No that happened some time ago.

So, you're already 'Chief Librarian'?

Not any longer. I changed from 'Chief Librarian' to 'Information Manager' when the bar-coding on periodicals was introduced.

And that's what you'd like in the minutes?

Not quite. Following the abolition of the Audio-Visual Centre, the University has now agreed that I should become 'Director of Learning Resources'.

Well, I suppose congratulations are in order.

Most thoughtful.

May we now forge ahead with the allocations. We completed Palaeontology last Friday, so it's straight on to Physics. We have a long, slightly self-serving letter from the Head of Department which outlines research and teaching developments in such 'key areas' as Geo-Physics, Plasma Physics, Magnetic Multi-Layers, and something which seems to be called Nanoscopic Studies.

All very interesting, Madam Chairman. But how does 'Physics' measure up on our rating system?

If we apply the standard criteria to this bid, then Physics emerges with 27.5 points, which puts it clearly in the Medium category.

Bang in the middle?

Sort of Upperish Medium.

I must say I find that generous. Physics does have a slightly old-fashioned sound to it. Surely we should be directing our resources to more modern subjects such as Quality Management.

Is that view shared?

I certainly think Physics might come down to the Lower Medium category. Even verging on the edge of 'Small'. Perhaps though, Madam Chairman, we should err on the side of generosity. After all this coming Monday does see the start of National Library Week.

We're agreed then. Next year, the Department of Physics will, subject to all normal library committee guidelines, be allowed to buy one small to medium sized book.

7 Exam marking

Department of Media and Cultural
Studies

21 June 1993

Dear Professor Dowtidge

I'm writing in my capacity of Examinations Officer to provide
you with some background information on a few of the disputed finals papers which we are now pleased to enclose for your adjudica-
tion.

Candidate 518247 Spooner J.
Examination: Linguistic Theory

As you will see the internal markers have a serious disagreement here.
Dr Piercemüller has awarded a mark of 57, while Dr Quintock prefers
an 82. It is perhaps relevant to this case, although I only mention it
for guidance, to say that Dr Piercemüller has this year displayed what
might be called statistically abnormal predilection for the mark of 57 –
having awarded it to 39 out of the 42 papers which have fallen under
his purview.

Candidate 529186 Dubbins S. K. (Miss)
Examination: Dadaism and After

Although this candidate has performed well elsewhere in her finals
papers she appears in this instance to have taken advantage of what
her internal examiner called 'a tendency within the subject matter'
and submitted eight pages of 'automatic writing'. At first the internal
examiner was inclined to rate this as an overall Pass (principally on
the grounds that it was relatively long *and* laser-printed) but Professor Lapping subsequently undertook the complex task of comparing
Miss Dubbins' work with an earlier example of the genre conceived
by a Ms Gertrude Stein. His feeling after this exercise was that Miss
Dubbins certainly merited a Lower Second and Ms Stein a borderline
Third.

Candidate 543172 Bocock N. V.
Examination: Base and Superstructure

This particular paper raises a rather serious issue in that it was originally marked by Mr Ted Odgers, who now, on ideological grounds
related to the recent pay dispute, refuses to release his mark. (I should
say that this is a localized problem in that Mr Odgers has only this
one student on his present 'Base and Superstructure' course.) It's dif-

ficult to know how best to proceed in the circumstances. Dr Quintock does claim to have seen the phrase 'Remember '68' written in large letters in Mr Odgers' desk diary but given Mr Odgers' historical interests, this may well refer not to Bocock's paper but to the 'events' of 1968. Professor Lapping has, however, now proposed that we proceed on the assumption that the paper has been marked by another internal examiner – namely, Dr Piercemüller – and that it therefore be regarded as a 57. We look forward to your comments on this sensitive matter.

I think all the other 27 problem cases which I'm forwarding to you along with these remarks are self-explanatory, and I very much look forward, as do all my colleagues, to seeing you at our Examiner's Meeting the day after tomorrow.

Best Wishes

L. Turpitz (Examinations Officer – still)

8 Modularisation

Oh, Maureen. Sorry to bother you. But I'm having trouble with my timetable. My name's Buzzard. Adam Buzzard.

As in buzzard?

That's right.

And your problem?

It's my first year seminar group for the A2 Communication course.

Butler, Buttress, Buxom – yes, here we are – Buzzard. Adam Buzzard. You've chosen six first year modules in Media and Cultural Studies with additional first term modules in Creative Accounting and Palaeontology.

That's it.

And for the A2 Communication course you're in seminar group 46B. Tuesday mornings at 10.15 in the Xerox room.

And that's my problem. It clashes with my Palaeontology.

Then Palaeontology must be a 'D' list module. If you're taking any of the 'A' modules then you can only choose other outside modules from lists 'A', 'B', or 'C'.

But Palaeontology is a 'C' list module. Look.

Then how about moving from Group 46B to Group 23A which meets at the same time on Wednesday morning?

That clashes with my Semiology.

Buzzard, I want to ask you a serious question. What made you choose Palaeontology as an outside module?

I was interested in fossils and what they tell us about the history of the world.

Listen, Buzzard, Adam. I'm going to speak very frankly. The only fossils you'll encounter in our department of palaeontology are on the teaching staff. They are seriously dull.

Really?

Oh yes. Listen, Adam. Ever wandered across the countryside in springtime and thought how beautiful it looks?

I suppose so.

All those pretty flowers you can't quite put a name to.

Well, yes.

Then listen, Adam. Forget Palaeontology. Dusty old dead fossils. Boring old courses. Look what I've done. I've popped you down for Botany. Nice course. Nice people. Pretty flowers. And on a Tuesday morning at 11.15. What could be better?

Gosh, thank you, Maureen.

Think nothing of it. It's what student choice is all about.

9 The decline in academic standards

Concern is being expressed that academic staff are concealing falling standards – THES

Dr Quintock will now commence his presentation.

Thank you, Professor Lapping. My brief this afternoon is to demonstrate the critical percentage changes which have occurred in the factors related to undergraduate teaching in the last two decades. May we please have Slide One.

TEACHING STAFF	
1973	1993
27	5

Here you see what amounts to an 81.5 per cent fall in the number of tutors actively employed in undergraduate work in this department in the last two decades. Slide Two please.

SEMINAR GROUPS	
1973	1993
6	24

These figures document the 300 per cent increase in the size of our undergraduate seminar groups during the same period. Slide Three please.

LIBRARY EXPENDITURE	
1973	1993
£4.25	8p

And here we see the 98 per cent reduction in the average amount of expenditure per student by the central library facilities. Slide Four please.

DEPT. DEGREE RESULTS		
	1973	1993
Standard 1st	1	6
Firsts	2	12
Upper 2nds	26	63
Lower 2nds	31	6
Thirds	8	0

And here we have an across the decades comparison of the proportionate change in degree results. Notice the 500 per cent increase in both starred and unstarred firsts, the improvement of 142 per cent in upper seconds, with lower seconds falling by 81 per cent and thirds by a whole 100 per cent.

These dramatic improvements in our degree profile need then to be seen in the context of the previously demonstrated declines in library funding, staffing and increases in seminar size. They are improvements which I suggest could only have been achieved by a department like our own which

was totally committed to Britain's
newest principle of higher education
– Slide Five please.

```
FIDDLING THE
ASSESSMENT
SYSTEM
```

Slide Six please.

```
THAT'S ALL
FOLKS!
```

10 Coping with postgraduate life

A recent British survey found that nearly all postgraduates were dissatisfied with their experience – THES

Dr Piercemüller?

A student? At the end of July? Shouldn't you have gone home long ago? No point hanging around the corridors you know. You won't get a degree that way.

I've got a degree. I'm a postgraduate. I'm John Gribble. And you are my supervisor. I've been trying to see you since I arrived last October.

Well, you're seeing me now, Gribble. So, no need to labour the point. I take it you've no other worries.

Nothing much more than inadequate supervision and sitting in a crowded room for two hours a week listening to tired old lectures on research methods.

Let's not forget the seminars.

Going away in groups of ten and reporting back with comments on the tired old lectures?

It's called 'independent learning'.

And then there's the teaching we have to do.

You mean the opportunities we provide for you to gain some experience in your likely career.

I mean not being given a single day's training before being plunged at £7 an hour into taking eight first-year seminar groups a week.

Gribble, you obviously feel strongly about all this. Why not go away and write down your comments and then they can be considered a little more dispassionately.

I've written them down. I've written this ten thousand word essay on 'Academic Exploitation in the Modern University'.

That's it there? In your hand? Gribble, let's not part on this sour note. Quite frankly, now I think about it, I'd like to associate myself with some of your arguments.

You would?

Oh yes. Look, I'll just pop my name alongside yours on the title page. There it is. Piercemüller and Gribble. A nice ring. And now it's all ready for *The British Journal of Higher Education*. But, Gribble, before you pop it in the post ...

Yes?

Do take that word 'exploitation' out of the title. It's ever so slightly loaded. And have a splendid holiday.

And you, Dr Piercemüller.

11 The 'new' professors II

Dons at 'old' universities are concerned that the creation of so many professors at the 'new' universities is devaluing the academic title – THES

Maureen? D'you have a spare moment?

I might have one coming up next Sunday afternoon.

Because we need to drop a line to the poly about this damned business of sharing academic journals.

The City University of Poppleton.

Whatever. Better send it to that chap we wrote to last time. The one in the department of communication. Ted. Ted Boalerges.

Professor Boalerges?

What?

He's now 'Professor' Boalerges.

That fellow with the long greasy hair and the lumber jacket? Are you absolutely sure?

Couldn't be surer. When I rang him last week to say we'd be writing just as soon as you got back from holiday he picked up the phone and said 'Professor Boalerges speaking'.

The 'Ted Boalerges' who used to hang around with that hippy looking woman with the mongrel dog and the tattoo on her arm. Could hardly string a sentence together. 'Sue' something or other. Sue Grubbit.

Professor Sue Grubbit.

What?

It was in last week's *Evening Press*. Big picture. And a list of her hobbies.

One doesn't want to be too snobbish, but there surely must be some way in which proper professors could still be distinguished from, well, other professors?

There surely must.

You know, Maureen, I think it might help a little if you slightly changed the way you referred to me in public.

Anything you say, Professor Lapping.

I know it's a shade inflexible, but from now on, at least on formal occasions, would you mind awfully calling me Professor Professor Lapping?

What else?

APPOINTMENTS
UNIVERSITY OF POPPLETON

LETHAL VIRUS OFFICER

Applications are invited for this new position which has been established in order to maintain a constant check on extremely dangerous viruses which have recently been leaking from an area not unadjacent to the university's Department of Philosophy. These viruses are completely invisible but when ingested can incline otherwise perfectly normal lecturers to conclude that the present Vice Chancellor is a raving megalomaniac who has surrounded himself with a bunch of so-called managerial experts who couldn't run a hot dog stand (let alone a university) between them.

For an informal discussion about this post please contact Jim.

12 Academic meetings

Tuesday Afternoon Time Immemorial Committee

Minutes of the meeting held on 11 January

Present:	Professor V.S. Grappling (Chair)
	Dr Q.A. Spermhandler
	Dr D.T.W. Wratchet
	Mr L.S. Horsefountain
Also present:	J.W. Brooding
	L.A. Catchment
In attendance:	Miss I.J. Punting (Secretary)
Popped in for a moment:	T.H. Local
Noticeable by their absence:	Dr S.C. Pierpoint (Vice Chancellor)

Apologies received from Professor C.C. Gauntlet

94/1 Approval of the Minutes of the last Meeting

It was noted that the name of Professor Dingbat appeared in the list of apologies for the last meeting of this committee. After some discussion it was agreed that as Professor Dingbat was not in fact a member of this committee or indeed, as far as anyone knows, of the University itself, his 'Apology for Absence' should be deleted from the minutes.

94/2 Matters Arising from the Minutes

(a) Dr Spermhandler reported that since the last meeting he had been looking into one or two questions raised by the minute 93/126 but so far did not have any of the answers. After a detailed discussion it was agreed that no further action would be taken on any of these matters until after the committee had had the opportunity to hear further from Dr Spermhandler.

(b) Professor Grappling (Chair) reported that he had received a letter from Professor Dingbat complaining that he had not been sent a copy of the minutes of the last meeting of this committee. In view of 94/1 it was decided that no further action would be taken in this instance.

94/3 Jarratt Recommendations

Dr D.T.W. Wratchet explained to members of the committee that they would shortly be receiving a preliminary copy of his subcommittee's deliberations on a proposal from the Outside Speakers' Committee that the Jarratt recommendations on streamlining decision-making in university committees be declared 'inappropriate' for those committees which had within the last 10 years not made anything which would be recognised by any reasonable person as a decision. Dr Spermhandler thanked Dr D.T.W. Wratchet for the diligence he had displayed in detecting the imminent arrival of a report from his own subcommittee.

94/4 The Vice Chancellor
Following the departure of the student representatives, Mr L.S. Horsefountain raised the whole question of the Vice Chancellor.

94/5 Any Other Business
Mr T.H. Local asked for permission to point out to the committee that once again 'Any Other Business' had been confined to the end of the agenda, a position which ensured that any business raised under the heading would be likely to receive somewhat more cursory treatment than that tradition- ally accorded to business appearing at an earlier stage. After a detailed dis- cussion it was agreed by 4 to 3 (with 2 abstentions) that for a trial period of six years, 'Any Other Business' would now appear at the head of the commit- tee's agenda, immediately before 'Apologies for Absence'.

94/6 Death of Dr Q.A. Spermhandler
Miss I.J. Punting (Secretary) asked for permission through the chair to note that Dr Spermhandler had expired sometime during the second half of the present committee meeting. As it was now 5 o'clock it was agreed without division that this item would be placed on the agenda for the next meeting.

13 Visiting scholars

'The problem in this country of people shying away from foreign languages is becoming preposterous' – Professor Norman Stone on his plans to open a European Institute at Oxford in 1992 – THES

May we now move on to Item Six – 'Visiting Scholars'? Your baby I believe, Dr Quintock?

Not exactly, Gordon, but I'm very happy to say a few words about the matter.

Excellent.

Well, about three months ago, I received a letter from a university in France, the University of Toulouse. I don't know whether anyone has ever heard of it but I gather it's more or less straight down towards the bottom.

Slightly to the right.

Quite so. Anyway I received this letter from someone calling himself Professor Michel Larotte of the Department of Cultural Studies – in English that's plain Michael Larotte – in which he said he wanted to visit this department to see how we taught cultural studies to undergraduates.

Sounds a bit vague. Did he write in English?

No, I'm afraid he didn't. I got Maureen to knock up a quick translation.

Typical.

Quite so. But someone will have to look after him when he arrives next week. Quite frankly, I can't speak a word of the stuff.

If he doesn't understand English what's the point of him coming?

That's just it. We don't know whether he can speak English or not.

But he wrote in French.

Perhaps he was trying it on. Apparently lots of these French people can actually speak perfectly good English but deliberately pretend they can't just to make a point.

Well, I suppose we must cover ourselves on this one. Can anyone here speak French?

I'm a peu *rusty, Professor Lapping, but I think I could handle a couple of greetings. You know,* bon jour *and* bon matin. *'Good day' and 'Good morning'. Whichever you prefer.*

Certainly a start. Yes, Professor Dabsit?

I believe I might be able to manage the odd pleasantry. **Asseyez-vous, s'il vous plaît.** *That's 'Sit down, if you please'.*

Jolly good. Anyone else. Yes, Mr Odgers.

I can more or less order a simple meal. Deux cafés au lait et deux croissants. **That sort of thing.**

Most satisfactory.

In what way, Professor Lapping?

In that while it may prove difficult to give Professor Larotte a comprehensive view of our teaching philosophy, it would seem that by combining all our departmental linguistic skills – we're well capable of offering him a seated breakfast.

Vive la France.

This Week's Research Grants

Dr L.T Mincing, University of the South West of Shropshire, £1,100 from the DoH for a three month longitudinal study of acute anxiety patterns in untenured academics waiting for news about the relative success of their recent grant applications.

14 The university motto

From the Vice Chancellor's Office

Dear Colleague

As you will remember, I wrote to you in April 1992 with the results of a nationwide survey which revealed that, even when prompted, only 2 per cent of the UK population were aware of the existence of this university.

As a result of these findings the Planning Committee established the Sub-Committee on University Identity with a brief to 'look into the ways in which it might be possible to increase the public's awareness of the existence of this university and to report back'.

After wide-ranging consultation, the Sub-Committee produced an interim report in March 1993 which strongly suggested that we should 'seriously consider ways in which the present university motto – *Quam Bonum in Unum Habitare* – How good it is to dwell in unity – might be modified so as to bring its corporatist sentiments more into line with current individualistic and entrepreneurial values'.

As a result of this report all departments were asked to nominate alternative mottoes by September 1994. I now enclose the Sub-Committee's verdicts on the submissions which were received by that date:

Economics Department: Si nemo sequitur solus ibo – *If no one follows I will go alone.*
The sub-committee thoroughly appreciated the individualistic ring to this motto but found it somewhat negative in tone. As one member put it: 'Instead of suggesting that this university is full of leaders, it intimates that it is packed with followers'. *Five points.*

Biology Department: Ardua petit ardea – *The heron seeks the heights.*
Whilst admiring the ingenuity with which this proposal brought together the new individualism and current ecological concerns, the committee felt that singling out the heron in this manner was downright misleading. *Four Points.*

Sociology Department: Multi pertransibunt et augebit scientia – *Many shall pass through and learning shall be increased.*
The Sociology Department explained that the intention of their motto was simultaneously to take into account the increased numbers of students now entering higher education and counter the 'more means worse' viewpoint. The sub-committee commended the philosophy behind this submission but after discussion decided that the motto was ridiculously long. *Three points.*

Theology Department: Manent ultimain coelo – *The best things await us in heaven.*
It was felt by all members of the committee that whilst 'deferred gratification' remained a commendable middle-class imperative, this was taking things altogether too far. *Two points.*

In the circumstances the committee decided after prolonged discussion that there 'should be no immediate change to the present university motto'. However, in order that the recurrent themes of ecology, individualism, and entrepreneurialism might be more adequately represented in the university's visual identity, it proposed that instead of the motto appearing as it is at present across the pages of an open book, it will now run directly above the forepaws of a leaping badger.

I look forward to having your comments on this important issue by 26 October 1994. Letters should be sent directly to me and marked 'Badger'.

The Vice Chancellor

15 Timetabling

As it's just gone 11.20, perhaps we could make a start. Before I introduce our speaker, I wonder if some of you would consider filling up these empty seats at the front. Gentleman at the back. Yes, you. Do come forward. I take it you want this workshop.

I'm not absolutely sure.

Perhaps you could tell us what you were looking for.

I was rather hoping for Professor Dingwall on 'Post-Modernism and the Baroque'.

You're in quite the wrong building. This is 'The Globalisation of Culture' with Dr R Tizard.

This is Room 3065 in the Newton Building?

No, this is 3065 in Einstein.

But Einstein was where I had an inadequate breakfast this morning.

No, that was Darwin. Einstein was last night's badly organised 70's disco.

My apologies.

No problem. Yes, woman in third row?

Did you say this was 'The Globalisation of Culture' with Dr Tizard.

Yes indeed.

Not Professor Dopple on 'The Re-tribalisation of the West'?

No, Professor Dopple was here yesterday. You're in the right building at the right time but on the wrong day.

My apologies.

Right. May I now assume that everybody else knows roughly where they are. Excellent. So without further ado let me call upon Dr Tizard to introduce his paper. Dr Ralph Tizard.

Thank you very much. Most gratifying. I myself must start with a slight apology. For although I am a doctor and my name is Ralph Tizard there may have been some slight mistake in that my paper is not directly concerned with what I believe the chairperson referred to as 'Globalisation'.

It's not?

No, its precise title is 'The use of gene sequence divergence to determine the evolutionary history of streptomycete soil populations'. Would that still be all right? I rather need to deliver it somewhere.

Well, as we're now down to an audience of two it hardly seems to matter any more.

I'll be as brief as possible.

Why's that?

So as to leave more time for questions.

What else?

THE GRADUATE SCHOOL OF CULTURAL AND MEDIA STUDIES
AT POPPLETON PARTICULARLY WELCOMES APPLICATIONS
FROM RICH OVERSEAS STUDENTS WITH VERY LITTLE
COMMAND OF ENGLISH OR SENSE OF THE VALUE OF MONEY
WHO ARE CURRENTLY UNDER-REPRESENTED IN THE SCHOOL

16 Health and safety

Academics whose low research activity 'caused' a rating of below '5' for their department may be given health and safety duties – Letter to staff from the provost of University College

Are you alright on 'resuscitation', Maureen? No trouble with the spelling?

I'll have a stab at it, Professor Lapping.

Excellent. On we go then. Point Six.

Point Seven.

Is it really? Right. Point 7. Now how shall we phrase this? Ah yes. 'If, despite mouth-to-mouth resuscitation, the patient starts turning a blue-grey colour, then immediately start heart massage taking care not to be too violent in case you break a rib'. New heading and new paragraph.

With the heading in bold as before?

Exactly as before. '**Fire Procedures.** As Health and Safety Officer you are also responsible for taking immediate actions in the event of a fire. These actions are as follows'. Semi-colon.

Is there a list to follow, Professor Lapping?

There is indeed.

Then would perhaps a colon be more appropriate?

Try not to be pedantic, Maureen. It doesn't suit you. 'If you discover a fire, immediately operate the fire alarm call point. Then attack the fire with the nearest appliance'.

Might it not be clearer if one said 'nearest fire appliance'. In that 'the nearest appliance' might well be, say a board duster?

'Nearest fire appliance. Then tell all persons to immediately proceed to the Assembly Point in the Head of Marketing's private car park'.

Splitting their infinitives as they go.

New paragraph. 'I hope all is clear and that if you have any specific problems you will not hesitate to consult me before taking up your new duties as Health and Safety Officer next Monday morning. Yours etc.' You can't think of anything I've left out.

Only the mild hope I mentioned earlier.

What mild hope?

The mild hope that when a departmental emergency does occur, Dr Piercemüller encounters no serious hold-ups at Pisa airport.

That will be all for today, Maureen. It doesn't suit you.

This Week's Research Grants

Dr Dorothy Topiary, Institute of Renaissance Artifacts, the Open University of Milton Keynes, £1,950 from the British Academy for a computer analysis of the number of lines in the early Shakespearean canon which begin with the letters 'A' and 'B'. (This could go on for years.)

The University of Poppleton
(in association with John West – 'Insist on the Best' – Tuna)

DEGREE DAY 1994
Bill of Fayre

Your Degree Scroll
Choose from:

Genuine Egyptian Papyrus	£55.50
Hand Tooled Vellum	£45.50
Xerox 2000	£12.50

Your Degree Day Photograph
Choose from:

Head and shoulders (passport size)	£12.50
Full-length	£22.50
Full-length with Vice Chancellor	£35.50
Full-length in Academic Setting	
(Library background and life size cut out figures – choose from	
Einstein, Wittgenstein, Michael Ignatieff)	£55.50

Recording of Degree Ceremony

Double-sided cassette	£15.00
LP	£22.50
CD	£27.50
(Disco Mix version of any of the above add £5.00)	

Video Recording of Degree Day

Ceremony High Definition Nicam Stereo Version	£175.00
Professor Lapping's hand-held CamCorder	£35.50

Special Degree Day Buffet

Bowl of Strawberries and Cream	£14.50
Bowl of Strawberries	£12.00
Pick Your Own Strawberries	
(Apply to Maintenance Officer)	£8.50
Gown Hire: Designer Gowns are Available as Below	
Chinese Raw Silk	£255.50
Cotton Mixture	£120.50
Crimplene	£65.50

(Please add 20 per cent to all above prices for higher degrees).

How to Get There

Please note that the Degree Day Ceremony will take place in the Grand Hall (formerly the Central Library) and that parents and friends of graduands should be seated at least one quarter of an hour before the proceedings commence at 3.30pm. Please observe the following seating arrangements:

Front Stalls Reserved for parents of graduands with first class degrees

Rear Stalls Reserved for lower-second parents

Standing at the side Third class parents and Diploma of Education parents

Degree Day 1994 is produced and directed by Transworld Corporation
Cigarettes by Abdullah
Ceremonial Mace and Chain by Ratners

APPOINTMENTS
UNIVERSITY OF POPPLETON

FLAG DAY CONTROLLER
(Trays)

£45,000 (+ commission) Following the resignation of Emeritus Professor Bostock, we are now seeking an experienced Flag Day Controller to take sole responsibility for the design, distribution and storage of trays in connection with the university's bi-monthly Flag Days ("Buy a Poppy for Poppleton"). The successful candidate will liaise with the Assistant Controller of Flags and the Deputy Director of Tin Cans.

18 Falling student numbers

Maureen, are you tied up at the moment?

Not at all, Professor Lapping. I was simply idling away a few minutes collating 250 finals scripts, teaching the rudiments of Word 5 to Dr Quintock, sending out a reminder that no one has yet paid their £10 towards the Examiner's Dinner, and trying to revive Dr Piercemüller's rubber plant.

Jolly good, Maureen, you know about students don't you? Undergraduates. That sort of thing.

Know about students, Professor Lapping?

Well, know about their little problems. You see them around. In the offices and corridors.

I suppose so.

And how are they, Maureen? Are they happy with the department? With the courses? With their lives?

Not what I'd call 'happy'.

What seems to be the trouble?

I don't want to be dogmatic about this.

Of course not.

But I'd say that between 25 and 30 are seriously disturbed at finding that 'an emphasis in the department on small group teaching' means a fortnightly seminar with 18 other students.

Seriously disturbed?

I'd say so. And round about the same number are dangerously depressed by the lack of feedback on their essays and projects.

Dangerously depressed?

And I'd say a good dozen are positively suicidal about their accommodation problems.

Positively suicidal?

And five or six are already displaying signs of chronic malnutrition.

Malnutrition?

That's right.

So that's about 80 students with some sort of grumble? Any overall observations to add, Maureen?

None at all, Professor Lapping. I was only wondering if you're now ready for me to go on to the second years.

19 The business school

THE UNIVERSITY OF POPPLETON
Institute of Business Studies
(purveyors of high class business courses to the business community since May 1994)

MASTERS DEGREE IN BUSINESS ADMINISTRATION (M.B.A.)
choose from the following options

One year
FULL-TIME
course with three terms' attendance at the Institute of Business Studies.
Fees: £25,000 (does not include residential costs)

Two year
PART-TIME
course with at least 90 days attendance at the Institute of Business Studies.
Fees: £20,000 (does not include residential costs)

One year full-time
SURROGATE
course which allows nominee of your choice to take the course for you, subject to the usual attendance requirements
Fees: £30,000 (does not include postage and packaging)

Three year
CORRESPONDENCE
course with no attendance requirements
Fees: £15,000 (does not include postage and packaging)

Three year
SUBLIMINAL
course with no attendance requirements
Fees: £15,000 (includes tapes suitable for use under standard size pillows)

Three year
0898 TELEPHONE
course with no attendance requirements
Fees: Calls charged at 34p per minute cheap rate, 45p at all other times

Special non-residential
UNDER-ACHIEVERS
course for all those who quite fancy an MBA but have never had anything remotely approaching a proper education
Fees: £35,000 (allow 14 days for delivery of signed degree)

Special Offer While Stocks Last:
Collect any ten of these advertisements from THES and complete the slogan below and you could win a 10% discount on any of the above courses (subject to availability):

'It's nice to see yet another university trying to cash in on the MBA market because ...'

20 The internal complaints procedure

'In the wake of the Donnellan case universities will examine internal complaints procedures for cases which bring the university into disrepute' –
Sunday Times

Ah, Lapping, old chap. Good to see you. I take it you know the university solicitor?

Yes indeed.

Look here, Lapping. I asked you to pop in today because of some disparaging references to this university which have recently appeared in *The Poppleton Evening Press.*

Disparaging?

On 28 October, for example, there was a letter signed 'ratepayer' which referred to Poppleton University admission policy as 'based on principles only previously tested in the design of the Black Hole of Calcutta'.

Good Heavens.

And on 3 November, another letter, this time from 'Blue Eyes', referred to this university's recent decision to opt for modularisation as yet another instance of the 'abdication of intellectual principles in favour of mere administrative convenience'.

Extraordinary.

And then in yesterday's edition we find a letter from a 'Man O'The People', which purports to agree with both 'Blue Eyes' and with 'Ratepayer' by arguing that such decisions are not unexpected in a university, and I quote, 'which is currently overseen by a Vice Chancellor whose highest ambition would be to have sole charge of a large biscuit factory'.

Almost unbelievable.

Lapping, I have reason to believe that you are not only 'Ratepayer' but also 'Blue Eyes' and 'Man O'The People'. What do you have to say?

I deny all charges.

In that case the university solicitor and I will have to refer your case to the University Complaints Committee.

Of course.

And I'm now pleased to be able to tell you that the University Complaints Committee has concluded its discussions and finds you guilty of at least two charges. You are accordingly fined £1,000. Have you anything you wish to say?

I was rather wondering if ...

Speak up, Lapping. It's your constitutional right.

Well, I was rather wondering if, in its wisdom, the committee might allow me some time to pay.

21 Overcrowded seminars

FURTHER DEVELOPMENTS IN STUDENT THROUGHPUT TECHNIQUES: SEMINAR DENSITY CONTROL

Choral Speaking

According to Gabstreet and Lodestar in the *British Journal of Experimental Overcrowding* (Vol 23. No.16 pp 233-274) considerable time may be saved in crowded seminars devoted to relatively familiar topics if instead of individual students being asked for an answer, the group is required to give the correct response in unison. Using three questions derived from different disciplines – a) What was George Eliot's first name? b) What is Boyle's Law? c) What were the seven causes of the French Revolution? – the researchers found that choral answers saved an average of 8.23 minutes in a one hour seminar.

Advanced Register Taking

Hassock and Tidypurse report in the February edition of the *Quarterly Journal of Student Processing* (Vol 4. No 2. pp 4-5) that the time-consuming practice of calling the register in seminars may now be a thing of the past. In a series of trials in three northern universities they persuaded 150 students to sew personalised bar-codes onto the back of their jeans. These were then electronically read as the students entered the seminar and provided the tutor with instant VDU access to absentees.

Ergonomic Advances

Pristine, Oakshott and Cantwell report in this month's *British Journal of Educational Furniture* (Vol 42. No 2. pp 17-165) that there has now been a wide take-up of their patented Bunk Seminar Seat (BSS). This essentially follows the principle of the bunk bed with a short ladder connecting the lower to the upper seat. The BSS not only makes use of wasted vertical space (VS) but also provides the tutor with a valuable way of acknowledging excellence.

Accelerated Questioning

Valuable minutes are frequently lost in crowded seminars when individual students who have nothing to say but whose names are among the few known by the tutor are repeatedly asked if they have any questions. Lamartine and Dentrite in *Recent Advances in Robotic Learning* (Vol 14. No 6. pp 136-160) describe a novel solution to this problem in which students who think they may have a question are asked before entering the seminar to take a numbered ticket from a roll attached to the tutor's door. When their number appears on the screen above the blackboard they are called upon to speak. The authors suggest this is a more pedagogically sophisticated technique than that proposed by Cockshott and Larkspur (1989) which simply used a show of hands to divide students into two groups: a Red Talking Channel and a Green Talking Channel. They conclude, however, that more research is needed if their department is ever to improve upon its present '3' rating.

This Week's Research Grants

Professor D.G.W. Stipend, University of Grantchester, yet another huge lump of money from somewhere in Europe for a rolling programme of research into the positive and enduring relationship between the promotion of individual academic careers and the exploitation of junior (and uncredited) researchers on short-term contracts (Stipend's Law).

22 University league tables I

LETTERS TO THE EDITOR

From the Vice Chancellor of the University of Poppleton

MADAM – I wish to protest in the strongest possible terms about the recent proliferation in the national press of so-called 'league tables' of universities based solely upon such notoriously ambiguous criteria as 'Expenditure on Books', 'Entry Standards', 'Staffing', and 'Research'.

The manifest nonsense of such exercises is nowhere more evident than in the case of my own institution – the Old and Ancient University of Poppleton – which, despite enjoying the highest academic reputation among lots of people I could mention, appears in 97th position in the most recently published list of 'Best Universities'.

This absurdly low placing is a direct consequence of the failure of the compilers of such tables to take into account other highly relevant criteria for assessing the excellence of a modern university. The present league table has, for example, no weighting for 'staff experience', an omission which clearly discriminates against Poppleton, where for many years we have prided ourselves on our ability to provide work, shelter and hot soup for more staff over the age of 55 than any other university in the country.

But this is not the only evidence of the selective manner in which the league has been assembled. As you will see below, Poppleton University also occupies leading positions in tables which address other critical aspects of university life:

Universities which are nearest to a good chip shop

1 University of Salford
2 University of Bradford
3 University of Poppleton

Oldest Universities beginning with the letter 'P'

1 University of Poppleton
2 University of Portsmouth
3 University of Paisley

When these new criteria are taken into account the current league table of Britain's top universities reads as follows:

1 University of Cambridge
2 University of Oxford
3 Imperial College
4 University of Edinburgh
5 University of Poppleton (Old and Ancient)

All of us at Poppleton are naturally gratified by this high placing but you have my assurance that we will not rest on our laurels. As I like to say over and over again on Degree Day: Only Number One is Good Enough for Poppleton.

Yours sincerely

VICE CHANCELLOR
(Ranked seventh in the 1993 CVCP Yard of Ale contest)

23 The university library II

From the library computer

14 September ... 1994

Dear ... *Professor Lapping* ...

Thank you so much for sending me your list of essential and reserve books for your ... *Autumn* ... term course entitled ... *Language, Culture and Identity* ...

I am now pleased to write to you, ... *Professor Lapping* ..., with the following detailed information on current availability of each of your selections:

1 C. J. K. Uttley **Modern Linguistics. Vol. 1. 1990.** *Out of print*
2 W. Cartwright **The Quest for Meaning in the Modern World.** *Cannot trace*
3 T. J. Guthrie **Essence and Existence.** *Missing from stacks*
4 L. Dibble **Personal Identity in the Contemporary World.** *Unknown*
5 C. V. Tomkins **A Sense of Belonging.** *Not at this branch*
6 L. Ketelby & D. Wilcox **Discovering Hermeneutics.** *Cannot trace*
7 D. G. Dobie **Whither Baudrillard?** *On very high shelf*
8 T. White & L. Harper **Ethics and Integrity in Cultural Studies.** *Damaged*
9 P. Slocombe **First Principles of Derridean Analysis.** *Fatal Error*
10 R. J. Titlake **Chaos Theory in the Social Sciences.** *Binding*
11 W. Litvarsky **Lacan's Law of Sexual Desire.** *Not available to students under 18*
12 P. Loat & J. Kirsky **Reformulating the Death Wish.** *On loan to chief librarian*
13 B. Pascal **Pensées** *Incomplete reference*
14 G. Lapping **Beat me Daddio: Popular Music 1934-7.** *Deleted*

As you will see from the above, this means that the number of books on your reading list which will be available from stock for next term is ...0...(nought). I am delighted to tell you that all these books will now automatically be transferred to the library reserve list and held there awaiting student requests.

As you will also see, there are unfortunately ...14... selections on your list which for various reasons have not been possible to locate. Under no circumstances,... *Professor Lapping* ..., should these be included in any of the reading lists you make available to students.

I do hope that all this will be helpful to you in organising your bibliographic requirements for the forthcoming term. Do let me know if there is any further way in which I can be of use.

Yours ... sincerely ...

The Library Computer

Wear your colours

Make sure that they know you're from the real University of Poppleton and not the jumped up Poly down the road. The University of Poppleton is proud to offer a limited edition of authentic reproductions of the university gown and hood. These facsimiles sturdily woven in hardwearing
Duritex are perfect in every detail. **£22.50**
(state chest and neck size)
Away strip also available

24 Absenteeism

Hello. Hello.

Department of Cultural and Media Studies.

Hello. Hello.

Department of Cultural and Media Studies. Is that you Dr Piercemüller?

Hello. Hello.

Dr Piercemüller, why don't you speak to me?

Good Heavens, is that you, Maureen?

It has been for some time now, Dr Piercemüller.

Thank God I've got through. Through at last.

Where are you, Dr Piercemüller?

Heavy drifting.

Pardon.

Phone lines are down at home. Three-hour battle to reach public call box. Must speak quickly. Wife and children alone. Blizzard on the way.

On the way where Dr Piercemüller?

On the way *here*, Maureen. What's the matter with you today?

Ah.

Possibility of being trapped. Night in 'phone box. Not discovered till morning. Relatives in shock.

Good heavens.

Listen carefully. This may be all I have time for. Cancel all, repeat all seminar groups and lectures until further notice.

Cancel all ...

Quickly, Maureen. Even now the drifts are rising.

All seminars and lectures. Yes, I've got that.

Send apologies: Departmental Committee, Admissions Committee, Faculty Board, Appraisal Workshop, Technical Staff Sub-Committee, Jarrett Recommendations Working Party.

Working Party. Yes, I've got that, Dr Piercemüller.

Blizzard closing in. Black ice. Abandoned vehicles. Prisoner in own house.

Dr Piercemüller, just one thing before you go.

Quickly. Quickly!

Would you like me to drop in your mail on the way home today? Like I did last time.

You don't catch me twice with that ruse, Maureen.

Tomorrow then?

That'll be fine.

Right you are. Bye, Dr Piercemüller.

Bye, Maureen.

25 Teaching large classes

Teaching Large Classes. Edited by Graham Gibbs and Alan Jenkins. – Title and details of book reviewed in THES

Other recent publications.

Filling in Endless Research Assessment Forms. Edited by Deidre Gradgrind and Mike Rote.
A thoroughly readable and informed guide to some of the more unexpected pleasures of completely pointless activities. Includes chapters on 'Putting your departmental publications into strict alphabetical order', 'Distinguishing between almost totally similar requests from the HEFC and CVCP', and 'How to rub your stomach and scratch your head at the same time'.

Getting to Grips with Twenty-Five Hours a Week of First Year Teaching. Edited by Luke Dobbin and Sarah Plodding.
A strongly recommended text for all those newly appointed short-term contract bottom-of-the-scale junior lecturers who are faced with a refreshingly heavy load of first year teaching. Includes chapters on 'Marking essays in bed: an overview', 'Understanding the problems of higher paid staff with very little teaching experience', 'Just a year ahead: facing up to unemployment'.

Sheltering from the Rain Because of Holes in the Roof of Teaching Accommodation. Edited by Beryl Pangloss and James Patching.
This is the definitive guide to the day-to-day management of serious defects in higher education today. Includes chapters on 'Having fun with a cardboard box and six rolls of Sellotape', 'Basic umbrella work in seminars and tutorials', 'The bucket in the corner: problems and prospects'.

Realising that Once Again We're All Going to Get a Lousy Pay Deal. Edited by Les Blinker and Michelle Turncoat.
This is vital text for all those anxious to come to terms with the dramatic decline in the living standards of teachers in higher education over the past 15 years. Includes chapters on: 'Rug making for pleasure and profit', 'Blaming the union leadership', and 'Recent advances in self-flagellation'.

Coping with Megalomaniac Vice Chancellors. Edited by Geoffrey Tacit and Leonie Wheedler.
A fascinating do-it-yourself guide to some of the critical authority problems faced by many teachers in today's new higher education environment. Includes chapters on: 'Reconciling oneself to unfair dismissal', 'Understanding the value of totally arbitrary decisions', 'Patterns of obeisance in the modern university committee structure'.

26 Commercial sponsorship

Commercial sponsorship of undergraduatecourses on the increase – The Times

Professor Lapping, I wonder if I might clarify some points of nomenclature?

Certainly, Dr Quintock.

As I understand it, one of the consequences of this generous donation from the private sector will be a change in your own title from Professor of Cultural and Media Studies to United Biscuits Professor of Culture and Media Studies?

That is correct.

And the new Joint Degree sponsored by the private sector will be known as the United Biscuits B. A. in Cultural and Media Studies?

Not quite. The directors of UB – a most hospitable group, incidentally – preferred the simpler appellation, B.A. Cultural Studies and Biscuits.

Thank you.

Professor Lapping. A small point of order relating to the admissions procedure for this new joint degree. Obviously we're looking for people who're interested in cultural studies, whether at a theoretical or empirical level, but also for those able to demonstrate a significant interest in biscuits.

That's true.

But supposing, and I put no more strongly than that, supposing we were faced by an excellent student who lacked biscuit knowledge. There is after all, as I understand it, no 'A' level in Biscuits.

Isn't there one in cake?

I think not, Dr Quintock. I take your point, Mr Odgers, and I think in those circumstances we will allow ourselves to be guided by our co-interviewer who will always be from the biscuit side of things. Any more points?

I was wondering in a relatively off-hand way about the weighting of the Joint Degree. As usual students are required to pass 16 modules but I notice the new stipulation that half of these modules must have a Biscuit ingredient.

That's very much to facilitate the development of other Joint Degrees. There are already indications that there might be some call for History/ Biscuits, English/ Biscuits, and even the PPB combination, Politics, Philosophy and Biscuits.

And do you envisage any end to this collaboration?

These are early days, but I believe that with the right commitment from all sides we might soon be talking about a Single Subject Degree in Biscuits, and with that the possibility, and I put it no higher, of a fundamental reorientation of our primary intellectual priorities.

You mean?

Exactly. We could become the first Department of Biscuits in the country.

UNIVERSITY OF POPPLETON
APPOINTMENTS

SENIOR LOGO
DESIGNER
c. £40,000

You will lead a small energetic team of six working on a new design for the University's shield and accompanying logo.

You will be sufficiently familiar with Logo Design to be able to resolve mythological and zoological contradictions which are inherent in the University's present depiction of a small dolphin leaping over a large rising phoenix.

---

27 The university video I

Sixth formers place least reliance on institutional videos in making their choice of university or polytechnic – THES

(Medium close up shot of man in corduroy jacket walking uncertainly towards the camera.)

Hello. As I'm the only personable looking professor on this campus who can read a cue card from ten yards without looking myopic I've been asked to present this video about the University of (insert name).

(Sudden cut to out of focus picture of distant molehills.)

As you can see we're lucky enough at (insert name) to be only a few miles away from some of the best scenery in this part of the country.

(Close-up of presenter's mouth and lower nostrils.)

But although Shakespeare claimed to find 'books in the babbling brooks' here at (insert name) there are also more traditional sources of knowledge.

(Close-up of wet concrete slabs.)

Here's our fine modern library. And here you see...
(We don't.)
 a typical group of undergraduates going about their studies.

(Cut to a typical group of postgraduates pretending to go about their studies.)

But life here isn't all work. University, as our Vice Chancellor explains, is also a time for finding out new and often surprising things about yourself.

(The Vice Chancellor is discovered sitting precariously on the edge of his desk. He speaks..)

You know how life at university isn't all work. It's also a time for finding out new and often surprising things about yourself. A time for finding out what you want to do when you go out into the broader world. A time for developing new leisure interests. A time for listening on ceremonial occasions to long rambling speeches by me in which sentence after sentence starts with the phrase 'a time for'.

(The Vice Chancellor continues to speak in medium close-up for eight minutes. At last we cut back to presenter who now has much longer hair.)

Thank you very very much, Vice Chancellor. But, you know, you don't need to take my word or the Vice Chancellor's about this university.

(Vice Chancellor alarmingly reappears in shot for a moment.)

Ask any of our former pupils – some of whom have gone on to become household names. People like Dave Scuddy, now lead guitarist with Trash the Pigs.

(Cut to picture of Malcolm Akehurst sitting behind a desk.)

Or Malcolm Akehurst, now a partner in the City.

(Cut to picture of Dave Scuddy, now lead guitarist with Trash the Pigs.)

Or better still ask any of the thousands of young people who have passed through these halls of learning.

(Picture of five or six people walking along a corridor.)

They know that when it comes to universities, (insert name) is tops. Tops for teaching, tops for research, tops for social life, and best of all ... er ... tops for everything else.

(The camera slowly tracks back to the muffled sound of another nail being driven into the coffin of the Director of Audio-Visual Studies.)

28 Equal opportunities

Universities ... have been condemned as among the worst discriminators against women; report by Hansard Society Commission

So we're agreed that Dr Cooper should be added to our shortlist?

I must say he looks a very solid sort of chap to me.

Very, very solid.

Solid and substantial. That's what I thought.

A nice overall sense of weight.

Excellent. So that's Cooper, Noakes, Sarney, Divott and Perkins. Five solid looking candidates. Should be able to fit them into a morning's interviewing. Any other names? Yes, Professor Fagan?

Well, Vice Chancellor, although I very much go along with your proposed short list, I wonder if we might just spend another couple of seconds on Dr Sangster?

Dr Janet Sangster?

That's right. You may remember that she was eliminated in the first round.

Quite so.

I only raise her name again because she does seem to have a very impressive publication record and three excellent references. On paper that rather makes her the equal of all our other shortlisted candidates.

Well, I can't see there being any great harm done if we were to take another peep at this case. Anyone else with strong views on Ms Sangster?

I have to say, Vice Chancellor, that I did go over her application with the proverbial fine toothcomb, but in the end decided, with some regret – God knows, we could do with some good women at the top – that there was, overall, something distinctly lightweight about her application.

A lack of solidity.

Not quite the degree of depth and gravitas one rather tends to look for in a departmental head.

A certain lack of bottom?

Yes, indeed. She somehow came through as a little too – a little too – insubstantial.

That's right. One would have welcomed a greater meatiness.

Well, gentlemen, how then might we best summarise our thoughts on this candidate?

I think, Vice Chancellor, that we should record our high opinion of this application – our very high opinion.

Hear. Hear.

But note that it was unfortunately somewhat lacking in – what might one call it?

Masculinity?

The very word.

42

This Week's Research Grants

Dr W.L. Turpitz, of the centre for the study of Contemporary Things, £31,234 from the Nuffield Foundation for a partisan investigation into patterns of nepotism in the refereeing of science research grant applications (1985-88) with particular reference to how Dr J.K. Fellowes managed to get such a fat grant from the SERC in 1987 (and *still* hasn't produced a final report).

29 Time management

Academics may be required to complete detailed reports showing how much time is spent on research – THES

Dr W.R. Keating, Lecturer in Psychology, University of Poppleton

Research Project: Contextual features influencing shock avoidance in rats.

Time sheet for Friday, 5 February

8 am to 9 am

Drive to university and park (29 min). Chat with Provost (15 sec). Remove car from Provost's space and park again (9 min).

9 am to 10 am

Arrive lecture theatre. Find plug for overhead projector (5 min). Start lecture on Theories of Learning (5 min). Pause while more students squeeze in (4 min). Continue lecture (12 min). Student faints (5 min). Complete lecture (29 min).

10 am to 11 am

Walk to laboratory and switch on lights (5 min). Ring Dr Milton and report escape of pigeon from Visual Discrimination Project (3 min). Chase and capture pigeon (11 min). Clean Skinner box in readiness for experimental trials (15 min). Phone call from Dept. Head requesting details of research papers published in last week (6 min). Remove experimental rat from home cage (3 min). Visit from members of University Research Quality Committee (15 min). Return rat to home cage (2 min).

11 am to 12 am

Meeting with Head of Dept. to discuss personal research goals and objectives for the next decade (45 min). Complete references for 17 former students (15 min).

12 am to 1 pm

Commence tutorial on learning theory (5 min). Welcome members of University's Teaching Quality Committee (8 min). Ask students questions on this week's topic (2 min). Wait for answers (15 min). Give brief lecture on this week's topic (30 min).

1 pm to 2 pm

Graduate supervision (45 min). Order rat food pellets (12 min). Eat own tuna and cucumber sandwich (3 min).

2 pm to 3.30 pm

Arrive laboratory and prepare Skinner box (10 min). Call from Dr Argyll re octopus (5 min). Roll up shirt sleeve in readiness for octopus feeding (1 min). Visit from members of HEFCE Quality Assessment Committee (50 min). Plunge right arm into octopus tank (15 sec).

Disentangle shirt from octopus (5 min). Remove rat from home cage (2 min). Place rat in skinner box (1 min). Telephone call from grant-giving body asking for interim report on research (14 min). Return rat to home cage (2 min).

3.30 pm to 5.30 pm

Dept Meeting to discuss student poverty (2 min), sexual harassment (3 min) and strategies for improving dept research rating in next round (115 min).

5.30 pm to 6.30 pm

Return lab and prepare Skinner box (7 min). Remove rat from home cage (2 min). Phone call from Head of Dept requesting today's research timesheet (3 min). Return rat to home cage (2 min). Prepare research timesheet (34 min). Ring Samaritans (12 min). Lights out in laboratory (30 sec).

30 Educational qualifications

CONFUSED ABOUT EDUCATIONAL QUALIFICATIONS?

Dr T.Q.M. Gumbril, reader in comparative qualifications at the University of Poppleton, answers your questions.

Q **I recently heard the Education Secretary, talking about starred A levels. What is a starred A level?**

A Starred A levels are an exciting new way of showing that although all sorts of riff-raff now get A levels, some candidates are, quite frankly, a cut above the others and so deserve a star. Starred A levels will be mainly used to gain entrance to starred universities (q.v).

Q **What happens when lots of people get starred A levels?**

A The Education Secretary will introduce a double starred A level.

Q **What are NVQs and GNVQs?**

A National Vocational Qualifications and General National Vocational Qualifications.

Q **Is NVQ like an A level?**

A Grade 3 NVQ is sometimes said to be a little like an A level.

Q **Is GNVQ like an A level?**

A A Grade 3 GNVQ is sometimes quite like an A level, so much so that the Government is now proposing to call it Vocational A level.

Q **You say that NVQ and GNVQ can be like an A level. Can they be like anything else?**

A There's no end to their versatility. According to the National Council for Vocational Qualifications, Level 4 GNVQs and NVQs are equivalent to diplomas or even degrees from non-starred universities.

Q **Doesn't it rather seem as though the whole system of NVQs and GNVQs might be a way of turning higher education into a much more vocational pursuit and thereby subverting the traditional academic role of the universities?**

A I'm sorry, but this column doesn't answer questions from conspiracy theorists.

Q **How competent is the average university admissions officer to deal with all these new qualifications?**

A Slightly below Level One NVQ.

Q **Thank you.**

A It's been an unalloyed pleasure.

31 Developing students' oral and presentation skills

Employers have asked universities and polytechnics to place more emphasis on cultivating student's oral and presentation skills – THES

Good morning, Seminar Group 14B. How are we all this morning?
How d'you like your first winter on campus?
Your college rooms warm enough?
And not too hot for you in here, is it? Well, I think everyone is present. So, shall we make a start?
Good. Well, this week you've all been looking at Max Weber's postulated relationship between the Protestant Ethic and the Spirit of Capitalism. So, let me start by asking if anyone would be so good as to tell me why they think Weber's argument might go some way towards undermining the type of economic determinism which has been associated with theorists in the Marxist tradition.
Anyone like to come in on that?
Anyone at all?
Julie?
Mark?
Roger?
Alison?
Michael?
Quite right. No point in running before we can walk. So, how about starting with a broad definition of what Weber meant by the 'Protestant Ethic'. Anyone like to come in on that?
Alison?
Julie?
Roger?
Michael?
Mark?
I see what you're all getting at. You're thinking that what we should start with is a definition of Capitalism. Right? Good thinking. Well, who'd like to help out with that definition?
Anyone at all?
Michael?
Mark?
Alison?
Roger?
Julie?
Jolly good. Well, that's almost it for this week. I think we've covered the main points. But just one last question to pull the threads of the seminar together. And do think before you answer. Would anyone here like to have a stab at spelling Max Weber's first name?
Anyone at all?

32 The student essay I

There is too much emphasis upon the student essay as a test of learning – THES

Before I start this essay I should say that the above statement is not very clear. It says 'there is too much emphasis upon the student essay', but it is not clear what would be 'too much'. Is it, for example, 100 per cent, which everyone would probably say was too much or 50 per cent, which some might think was not too much? This is, as already said, not very clear.

There are, however, several points in favour of 'the essay'. In the first place it is a good way of seeing whether people can put their ideas into order, and secondly it is a good way of showing if a person can write clearly although now that essays are often done on word processors and you can check spelling it is not such a good test of this any more. One of the most important things about an 'essay' is to make certain that it is tidy and quite long and has a bibliography. Then it will usually receive a large amount of ticks in the margin from the marker and 'very satisfactory' or 'promising work' at the end and a few other words that are difficult to read. Some people, on the other hand, say that 'the essay' is not any good because it is given too much emphasis. Speaking for myself I agree with this. Surely there are other ways of testing people like asking them to answer short questions or give them an oral. On the whole I would say that if you are going to have essays then they should not be in examinations but continuous assessment. In examinations it is easy to forget things because you've forgotten them or because they have become as Sigmund Freud said, 'repressed'. Freud was born in Moravia in 1856 and wrote many books including one of his best known ones about the future of religion.

Another point is that people have written essays in literature so it's not just something students do. There are some very good essays for example in *More Essays by Modern Masters* which we did at school. One of these essays was about Yorkshire by J.B. Priestley and there was another one a day in the life of a penny. One other thing about essays is that you can often do the same essay several times. Sometimes you do it for A level and then in the first year and then for finals. In conclusion, as I have hopefully shown, there are several things for and against essays. It is, as Marx often said, all quite dialectical.

P.S. Professor Lapping, I'm sorry this is difficult to read in places but I've been to the medical centre with an upset stomach.

33 Departmental duties

The Department of Cultural & Media Studies (University of Poppleton) proudly presents

Departmental Duties

HEAD OF DEPARTMENT	*Prof. Gordon Lapping*
CHAIR DEPT BOARD	*Dr Derek Quintock*
DEPT SECRETARY	*Maureen*
HEALTH & SAFETY OFFICER	*Dr Piercemüller*
	(on leave of absence)
SEXUAL HARASSMENT OFFICER	*(a.m.) Mr T Odgers*
	(p.m.) Dr D Quintock
RESEARCH INITIATIVES DIRECTOR	*Prof. Gordon Lapping*
PUBLIC RELATIONS OFFICER (UK)	*Mr T Odgers*
PUBLIC RELATIONS OFFICER (TUSCANY)	*Dr Piercemüller*
STUDENT COUNSELLOR	*Maureen*
STAFF COUNSELLOR	*Maureen*
DEPT DEVELOPMENT OFFICER	*Mr T Odgers*
PROJECTS TEAM CO-ORDINATING OFFICER	*Dr D Quintock*
GROUP GOAL FORMULATOR	*Prof. G Lapping*
CHAIR STAFF APPRAISAL COMMITTEE	*Mr T Odgers*
CONSTRUCTIVE FEEDBACK OFFICER	*Dr D Quintock*
LEARNING RESOURCES CO-ORDINATOR	*Prof. G Lapping*
TOTAL QUALITY ADVISOR	*Dr D Quintock*
ABSOLUTELY TOTAL QUALITY OFFICER	*Prof. G Lapping*
FUNDING COUNCIL LIAISON OFFICER	*Dr D Quintock*
COMPTROLLER GENERAL RESEARCH ARTICLES	*Prof. G Lapping*
FLAG DAY MARSHALL	*Mr T Odgers*
LOGO DESIGN & HERALDIC ARMS	*Maureen*
TEACHERS, RESEARCHERS, SUNDRY MINSTRELS AND MEN IN WHITE COATS	*Members of the cast*

AN HEFC PRODUCTION

34 The publisher's rep

Professor Lapping?

What is it, Maureen?

I'm so sorry to interrupt you when you're looking out of the window, but Rebecca Sarsted is here to see you.

Rebecca Sarsted? Ah yes. How is she?

As well as could be expected.

Good. Ah, Rebecca, there you are. Do take a seat.

Thank you, Professor Lapping.

Rebecca, let me start by saying that I've been here for thirty-three years. Thirty-three years, Rebecca. Practically twice the number of years you've been alive. Right? And during all those years, I've had a stream of people just like you coming to see me at exactly this time of the year with exactly your worries. Right? Worries about whether they have enough time for the job in hand. Worries about whether they will be able to do justice to themselves. Worries about their state of mind. Right?

I suppose so.

Rebecca, let's clear up one thing straight away. Don't worry about not sleeping too well. Right? Because the body can cope. Oh yes. We can all manage on far less sleep than we get every night so no need to worry about a few nights when you get less than the old eight hours. Right?

Right.

And, Rebecca, do remember that everyone else is in the same boat as yourself. All thinking that they won't do justice to themselves. But, of course, if everyone underperforms, then your relative position will remain exactly the same. Right? So no worries on that score. And do bear in mind that a little anxiety is a very good thing. Tests show that those people who don't feel anxious are the very ones who are likely to do least well. And, Rebecca ...

Professor Lapping?

Remember that it does all come to an end. Oh yes. There is light at the end of the tunnel. Tomorrow is another day. That's the good thing about the whole business. There's a date when it's all over and you can step back into the world again. And, Rebecca ...

Yes.

Do forget all those silly ideas about doing away with yourself. Put them right out of your mind. You see the thing is that those who spend a lot of time thinking that they might do away with themselves are the very ones who don't do it. It's as though thinking about it is a way of relieving the problem. Right?

I see.

And now, I want you to promise me one thing, Rebecca, will you promise to think very carefully about everything that I've had to say. Everything. Promise?

Certainly, Professor Lapping. But would it be alright if I didn't think about it at this precise moment?

How d'you mean?

It's just that I'm here to show you the new Macmillan catalogue.

35 Teaching assistants

CVCP's new initiative on teaching assistants – THES

Ah , there you are, Ms Thompson? Do sit down. How are the old MA studies coming along?

Not too badly.

You're appreciating Dr Quintock's course on Post De-Constructionism?

Oh yes.

And relishing Dr Piercemüller on Advanced Semiotics?

Well, I...

Excellent. Ms Thompson, let me come straight to the point. As you know we attach a great deal of importance in this department to developing the pedagogic abilities of our postgraduates and we've decided that you would be just the person to take over five or six weekly first year seminars on our Introductory Cultural Studies course.

Thank you, Professor Lapping.

Obviously we have to take your relative inexperience into account. So initially we'd be paying you the probationary honorarium of £5.25 per hour which would include such other minor tasks as overall assessment duties and informal supervision of students with learning or emotional difficulties.

Thank you.

Now, while we're on this topic, I seem to remember from your interview that you were pretty keen on Structural Linguistics.

I hoped there'd be a chance to pursue my interest in that area.

It's arrived. How about your very own second year undergraduate course on that precise subject? Just nine lectures a term, four seminars a week, and Bob's your uncle.

I'm not quite sure.

You're worried about the overall responsibility?

It's more a question of logistics. I'm not sure that I could fit all that teaching in with my postgraduate courses with Dr Quintock and Dr Piercemüller.

No problem, Ms Thompson. Such timetabling details would be up to you.

They would?

Oh yes. You see, in line with the CVCP initiative we're also proposing that you take over the teaching on the two postgraduate courses of which you are currently merely a member. Only from next term, you understand. No point in running until you can walk, eh?

I suppose not.

POLYGON Plc.

May we introduce ourselves? As the leading specialist company in the transformation of polytechnics into universities we are uniquely placed to offer advice on how to achieve your new corporate identity with speed and taste. All prices on request.

Thinking about a mace?

You should be. The mace is derived from the ancient metal-headed war club and there's no better way to say you've arrived as a university than to invest in this traditional mark of authority.

Choose between:

THE WAR CHIEF This 14ft long mace with solid club head and just the hint of an aggressive spike is not for the faint-hearted. Place this in front of you on degree day and hear the parents gasp. Strictly not for twirling!

THE ALL PURPOSE MINI MACE A folding mace specially designed for those who need to transfer their traditional symbol of authority quickly around the campus. It springs out to full length at the touch of a concealed button. Manufactured to high specifications in Bulgaria.

What are you doing about your Vice Chancellor's robes?

You're no longer a Principal but a Vice Chancellor. But here's the big question. To a Vice Chancellor are you a Vice Chancellor? Make sure the answer is a resounding 'Yes' by selecting **your** ceremonial robes from **Polygon**. All our robes are made from the finest material and lavishly decorated with lots of dangly gold bits.

Choose from the following styles:

The All Purpose King of Siam (as worn by Yul Bryner in **The King and I**).

The Classic Nero (as worn by Peter Ustinov in **Quo Vadis**).

The Full Length Eisenstein (as worn by Nikolai Cherkasov in **Ivan the Terrible**).

Now's the time to select your shield or crest

In the past nothing has so denoted the **real** university as a shield. In the words of one authority: 'Shields convey aristocracy, breeding and a general sense of being steeped in history'.

Our **shield** is bordered by a set of traditional heraldic supporters – a unicorn, two gerbils (rampant), and a sort of sea serpent with an olive twig in its mouth. In the centre is a galleon sailing on a wavy sea and below an open tome with the Latin motto **IGNAVUS NUNQUAM** (Never idle). The name of your university is then professionally steam-ironed into the space immediately below.

'Quite frankly, it's just the sort of thing we were looking for' – Vice Chancellor of the City University of Poppleton (formerly Poppleton Polytechnic).

37 Widening access

A new book by Sir Douglas Hague envisages a brave new world of 'star' professors using modern technology to reach wide audiences – THES

Ladies and gentlemen, undergraduates, graduates, access course and occasional students. It's exactly 9.30 am Greenwich Mean Time and I'm delighted to introduce today's video lecturer.

(Trickle of anticipatory applause.)

Will you please welcome someone who has long since left behind the mere parochialism of departments, faculties, or even universities. Ladies and gentlemen, will you please welcome one of our very first *World Professors.*

(Sounds of rising hysteria.)

Yes, here with the very latest white-hot developments in the area of media studies and popular culture – with particular reference to television and the family in the UK in the years between 1957 and 1963 –it's none other than your very own International Professor of Cultural and Media Studies, Professor Gordon – 'I Want to Teach the World to Think' – Lapping.

(Lights, drum rolls and fanfares. Enter Professor Lapping – for it is he.)

Good morning England, Scotland, Wales and Northern Ireland!

(Shouts of 'Give it to us Gordon'.)

Bon matin, Europe! Good evening, America! Good night, Australia! Good afternoon, Asia and Africa! Hello, World!!!

(Huge illuminated map to the side of Lapping's head glows with electronic hellos from around the world.)

I am delighted to be lecturing you this morning. *Je suis très content de vous parler ce matin-là. Me gusto mucho hablar con Vols esta mañana.*

(Shouts of 'Right on' and 'Viva Lapping'.)

Together with my fellow lecturers on this course, Claude Levi-Strauss, J K Galbraith, Jaques Derrida, and Noam Chomsky, I am proud, yes proud, proud to be associated with an educational venture which has no time for second-rate time-servers, proud to be part of an educational venture which truly takes us intellectually 'beyond universities'.

(Shouts of 'sack the lot of them – forward to the brave new world'.)

And now, without further ado, on with the real business of the morning.

(Shouts of 'Let's Go', and 'Allez'.)

If you'd all be so good as to turn to your interactive computers, we'll start straightaway – with the register.

38 Recruiting overseas students

'Honesty and truth should be the watchwords for recruiters for overseas students' – Strathclyde University conference on overseas students

Dear Mr Adobi

Thank you for your long and fairly interesting enquiry about the M.Phil course in the Department of Media and Cultural studies.

Let me say straightaway that we are extraordinarily enthusiastic about your potential application. Indeed, no sooner had your letter arrived than Dr Quintock, our graduate chairman, rushed into my secretary's office shouting: 'Gor blimey, Maureen, talk about a bit of luck. This could be another nine hundred nicker straight into departmental funds'. Let me, however, raise a few rather pedagogic points.

It is pretty obvious from your letter that you find it difficult to write in English. (Maureen and I didn't read it all that carefully but even so we discovered nine spelling errors, and one whole sentence which was utterly incomprehensible). This means that shortly after your arrival you will be required to join a large ill-organised English course run in a surly manner by a Language Department which clearly thinks it has better things to do with its time than help other departments pack in as many linguistically incompetent students as possible.

You mention that you are particularly interested in studying aspects of European post-war cinema with particular reference to Italian Post-Realism. That is certainly a fascinating topic but quite frankly nobody in this department knows anything very much about it except Dr Piercemüller who used to be a member of the National Film Theatre ('plenty of leg room but no Pearl and Dean' as he's fond of putting it). So, providing you have rather more luck finding him in the department than the rest of us have enjoyed over the past 23 years, it looks as though there should be no great problem over supervision.

On the social side, it's difficult to pretend that you'll find your fellow students on the course remotely congenial. Present day British graduate students lack any clear idea of what they want to do with their lives and are united by little more than a common possession of well-heeled parents. Most of them will be mildly embarrassed by your presence in the same room and will spend coffee breaks sitting together and giggling about your pronunciation, demeanour, or physical appearance. (Tutors will add to your general sense of alienation by employing a slightly louder voice whenever they ask for your opinions).

I hope that these comments will assist you in coming to a decision. If, however, you do write again, perhaps you'd be so good as to include a stamped addressed envelope – we're not made of money!

Yours according to Strathclyde guidelines,

Gordon Lapping

39 Setting exam papers

'Cultural studies is ... revelling in an extended adolescence, lashing out in all directions, inventing new concepts, along the way and celebrating its very refusal to meet the stifling demands of rigorous empiricism and laborious theory-making' – THES

UNIVERSITY OF POPPLETON

BA(Honours) Cultural studies

Answer as many questions as you fancy.

Time allowed: Round about three hours

1 Write brief notes on the cultural significance of any three (or four) of the following phenomena:
George Formby
The Yorkshire Ripper
Tony Slattery
Madonna
Adolf Hitler
The Queen Mother
Maltesers
Beavis and Butt-head
That recent advertisement for a bra which caused all the fuss

2 Invent a few facts which vaguely support the commonplace argument that Mills and Boon books can be analysed into a few basic themes.

3 With reference to not much more than your own ideological predilections prove either that pornography is essential-liberatory or exactly the opposite

4 Be briefly clever about Hitchcock's appearances in his own films.

5 Put your mind into neutral and free associate around any recent tracks by Take That.

6 Waffle on inconsequentially for about 1000 words on a cultural subject of your own choice.

7 Invent totally new concepts to explain any of the following issues in cultural studies:

a. The relative lack of post-modern reflexivity in 'Don't Forget Your Toothbrush'.

b. The rise and fall of grunge culture (try not to mention Kurt Cobain more than is absolutely necessary).

c. Why Jimmy Corkhill is messing around with cocaine in Brookside.

8 Cobble together a portentous sounding theory essay which *en passant* looks at people like Richard Hoggart, Stuart Hall, Raymond Williams, Roland Barthes, Dick Hebdige, Professor Gordon Lapping, Walter Benjamin (at least two paragraphs), Jean Baudrillard and Michel Foucault but totally fails to come to any recognisable conclusion (except perhaps that Baudrillard went a bit far).

This Week's Research Grants

Dr Piercemüller, University of Poppleton, £250 from Grindley Smoked Meats Plc ('You can taste the meat in Grindleys') for a one year study of the comparative preference among a random sample of Poppleton shoppers for Grindley Savory Pork Pies and Grindley Traditional Chicken and Ham Pasties.

40 The research assessment exercise I

I'm sorry to bother you again, Doctor.

That's what one's here for, Professor Lapping. Just lie back on the couch and relax.

Keep thinking about articles. Nothing but articles.

Tell me about these 'articles'.

You see, there was this research exercise and departments had to send in lists of articles so they could be graded and it didn't matter at the time because we all agreed the system was ridiculous.

Go on.

But when the grades came through all the people with good grades became very serious and started saying things like: 'Fortunately, we're a "four" or "Speaking as a five"'. And then everybody else joined in and began writing articles so that their department could be a 'four' and or 'five'. Articles disproving hypotheses no one had ever entertained, pedantic articles, inconclusive articles, articles really written by their research students. Any old article. New journals were founded to make spaces for even more articles. People who'd written lots of articles were hired so their articles could be added to the departmental total.

Go on.

And the perfectly normal hard-working people who hadn't written enough articles were told that they were deviants, that unless they immediately wrote more articles they were no longer welcome and should either leave or confine themselves to teaching.

Go on.

And when I said what we had all said before, that it was all a farce, that nobody needed so many articles, I suddenly noticed that they ...

Go on.

They were all looking at me as though I was the only one who'd gone crazy. Oh, Doctor, it was terrible.

Professor Lapping. I want you to know your problem is not unique. My colleagues have dealt with similar cases.

They have?

Oh yes. And on balance I'd say your anxieties very much fall into the clinical pattern we analysts have come to expect from what we call a typical 'two'. And now I must wish you a very 'good morning'.

Good morning?

Well, really, Lapping. I can't sit around here all day. Who else is there to write up your case for publication?

41 Modularisation II

May we now turn to item eight on the agenda: Introducing modularisation. Following the Vice Chancellor's decision that we must immediately adopt this very important development in educational theory, Dr Quintock has tabled some proposals. Any questions? Yes, Dr Turpitz.

I found some slight difficulty with Dr Quintock's extended pick 'n' mix metaphor. Am I to understand him as suggesting that our present three-year degree in cultural and media studies should be regarded as a bag of sweets?

Very much so, Dr Turpitz, but essentially a bag filled with different types of sweets.

Ah!

It might help to imagine our new modular students as moving along an academic counter taking scoops of fruit gums and Pontefract cakes and humbugs until they have assembled enough scoops to make a degree. If, as I propose, a degree has 16 modules, then each scoop of sweets selected is one of the ounces towards the graduating pound.

With structural linguistics as more or less the equivalent of a mint imperial and post-modernism as a coconut teacake?

Exactly so.

Might I raise another question? You say that there is also the possibility that scoops might be taken outside the cultural studies degree.

That's right. Two ounces of the 16 ounce cultural studies degree might be 'picked' from elsewhere. Perhaps from the philosophy department. Think of it as shopping at another counter with say, Kant, as a portion of Gruyère, and Heidegger as a slice of Lymeswold.

But I also understand the students may pick their sweets at a different shop. They might for example, select a scoop of chocolate drops from the City University of Poppleton and then drop into Poppleton University for an ounce of our liquorice all-sorts.

Exactly. You can pop in for an ounce one year and then collect another ounce 10 years later. As long as you get the final bag-full.

Good. Thank you, Dr Quintock. I think that explains the new system admirably. Admirably. Just one final point. As the person who has accepted the responsibility for implementing the modularisation scheme over the next six-and-a-half weeks and phasing it in with our existing degree, let me enter into the analogical spirit by asking if you'd all be so kind as to address your letters on the subject to 'the head of the fruitcake counter'. Other points?

42 The in-tray

Professor Lapping's in-tray

❑ Two DanAir tickets. Gatwick to Nice. Dated 4 August . ('Please note that flights are subject to unpredictable delays due to industrial action by French air traffic controllers'.)

❑ Two passports.

❑ One driving licence. ('Let's face it, darling, it's just so much simpler if one of us drives all the time and as I learnt to drive on the right last year it seems only logical'.)

❑ Twelve totally unmarked handwritten second year essays.

❑ Five seriously illiterate letters from school children asking for advice on their fourth-year projects. ('My form teacher said that you would be able to help'.)

❑ A second overweening request from the Vice Chancellor for a donation to the deputy bursar's retirement gift. ('I'm sure you'll agree with me that £18.30 hardly represents an adequate appreciation by colleagues of Mr Tidyman's work in the bursar's office for the past 32 years'.)

❑ Twenty-seven still uncompleted questions on social services reference form for a virtually unknown graduate. (Question 16. *In your opinion is this person suitable to be left completely unsupervised for long periods of time with extremely active young children?*)

❑ A three-quarter read MPhil thesis printed single-space on folded continuous sheet computer paper.

❑ A one-and-a-half page pedantic invitation to a colloquium in Leicester entitled: *Contemporary Cultural Studies at the Crossroads: Strategies and Counter-Strategies.* ('It is not our policy to pay any fees or expenses but the deputy college provost and his wife are generously prepared to offer the hospitality of their own home for your overnight accommodation'.)

❑ Three utterly unsolicited letters from Canadian academics enclosing off-prints of their recent articles in obscure North American journals. ('I eagerly look forward to receiving your comments on my paper'.)

❑ Less than half an apology from Dr Piercemüller for having to miss the first three weeks of the forthcoming autumn term on compassionate grounds ('the anticipated death of a fairly close relative').

(Professor Lapping is not quite yet on holiday.)

43 Marxism in academic life

Did you see all that stuff in the THES last week about Marxism?

What's that?

Marxism. In the THES. Last week.

Must have missed it. What was the general drift?

Well, roughly speaking, on the whole, Marxism was dead or dying in academic life.

Interesting.

Weren't you, yourself, once a bit that way inclined?

'Inclined'?

Towards Marxism.

Very loosely.

But didn't you used to sell papers outside the biscuit factory? *Red Torch* or *Red Flame*? Something like that.

One was peripherally involved.

All those headlines saying 'Smash the Bosses Now'?

There was some implicit criticism of managerial style.

And you had that Che moustache and the big boots and the T-shirt with that slogan – 'Paris, London and Turin. We Will Fight We Will Win'.

Berlin. Not Turin.

And wasn't it you who led that student torch-lit march across the croquet lawn to the admin block?

There may have been the odd torch.

With you at the front waving that red flag and shouting 'To the Winter Palace'?

I don't recall the flag.

And then occupying the Bursar's Office and declaring it a Red Base?

It was all essentially symbolic.

And all those concepts and ideas. Remember them: the proletariat, state capitalism, the control of the means of production, a class for itself, revolutionary consciousness, the withering away of the state, the communist nirvana? Whatever happened to all those? I suppose they've all gone the way of the torch, the flag and the moustache.

On the contrary. I retain them all as a matter of academic principle.

Principle?

The fundamental academic principle that one never knows when one's old lecture notes might come in handy.

44 Degree day III

And that, my Lord and Chancellor, Vice Chancellor, distinguished guests, honorary graduates, graduates, graduands, ladies and gentlemen, concludes the conferment of the degree of bachelor of arts in philosophy and corporate finance *magna cum laude*.

(Applause.)

Congregation will now proceed *secundum ordinem* to the conferment of the degree of doctor of philosophy *honoris causa*. I call upon Professor Gordon Lapping of the Department of Media and Cultural Studies at this university to introduce this year's candidate.

(General shuffling.)

My Lord and Chancellor, Vice Chancellor, distinguished guests, honorary graduates, graduates, graduands, ladies and gentlemen. As Erasmus succinctly observed, '*Quot homines, tot sententiae*' – 'there are as many opinions as there are men'. How very true. But how also very true that there are times when all opinions are as one, when there can be no argument about the genuine distinction achieved in life by one's fellow beings. Such is indeed the case with this year's candidate for a doctorate of philosophy of this university *honoris causa*: Kevin Bottomley – or, as he is now known both within and without his chosen profession – Funkmaster General.

Many of those who enjoy distinguished positions within our society reached the summit of their chosen profession only after long years of dedicated service. But, *ab initio*, from the beginning of his career, Funkmaster General took a different route. At the early age of 17 his musical genius was already being made evident in the series of rhetorical contributions he made to the emergent field of scratch 'an' rap – contributions which are perhaps best captured in the phrase used so eloquently by Petronious in his depiction of the spontaneity of Horace's verse – *curiosa felicitas*.

Others with less ambition might have been content with the achievements Mr Bottomley recorded in that primary field of cultural endeavour. But Funkmaster General was not one to stand still. Very soon he was found to be invoking the Virgilian precept, *audentes fortuna iuvat* – *fortune favours* the daring - and moving with the same degree of public acclaim – particularly in the West Midlands region – into other contemporary music genres. After a short and highly creative period in House, a period marked by such works as 'Doin that Thing', he was to be found very soon after in Garage – who now does not remember 'Keep it Comin'– and only recently completed the musical transformation to hip-hop.

My Lord and Chancellor, Vice Chancellor, distinguished guests, honorary graduates, graduates, graduands, ladies and gentlemen. In the past 250 years this ancient university has honoured many exceptional individuals – individuals chosen for their contributions to science and technology, the arts and humanities, and the social sciences. How appropriate, therefore, that this year we should be honouring in the person of Funkmaster General, someone who, while contributing absolutely nothing whatsoever to any of those areas, is still highly likely to get this university's name in the papers and thereby ensure a plentiful supply of undergraduates who might indeed choose any one of those areas.

(Applause and one or two indistinct shouts of 'Right on, baby'.)

45 Academic journals I

There is an urgent need to identify moribund academic journals – THES

The West Riding Journal of New Testament Studies Vols 4-412

Although scholars have regularly drawn upon such articles as 'Redundant Chapels in the Halifax Region' (Vol 227), this quarterly journal is now regarded by many leading edge British historians as far too generalist for its own good.

The International Journal of Vulgar Marxism Vols 1-234

This journal once played an important part in demonstrating the direct link between cultural superstructure and economic base. Matters no longer seem so simple.

Contemporary British Film Studies Vols 1-197

This journal has not regularly appeared in academic citations since its influential symposium edition on *The Lavender Hill Mob*.

The Cyril Burt Journal of Statistical Advances Vols 1-146

Although this bi-monthly has been regularly cited over the years by influential educational psychologists, it may now have fallen significantly below the critical level of probability.

The Eastern European Journal of Collective Farming Vols 1-1651

An unfortunate victim of the trend away from collective farming in Eastern Europe and the recent collapse of the entire Soviet empire. (v. also *Abstracta Yugoslavia*).

The English Journal of Arcadian Agrarian Society (incorporating 'Merrie England') Vols 1-146

Despite an invigorating Autumn 1992 edition entirely devoted to the wheelwright's art (with pull-out folk song sheet) this journal is no longer essential reading in departments of literature (or anywhere else for that matter).

Advances in British Manufacturing Vols 1-420

In engineering circles it is generally held that the reduction of this journal to a biennially published single duplicated sheet has somewhat vitiated its relevance.

The Comparative Journal of Meta-Narratives Vols 1-490

This respected journal provides regular reviews of the more popular meta-narratives (Christianity, Rationalism, Islam and The British Road to Socialism). The recent discrediting of all these meta-narratives (and others) by at least two French intellectuals has fatally undermined the entire subject area.

Developments in Heliocentric Thought Vols 1-1432

This attractively bound but fundamentally pre-Copernican journal has languished for some years despite its recent merger with the *The Proceedings of the Flat Earth Society* and *Monetarist Economics*.

46 Academic journals II

Britain's premier publisher of academic journals, Harcourt, Brace and Girdle, is pleased to announce three new journals specially designed for the New Age of Higher Education. (nb. In recognition of the modular accumulation and transfer character of contemporary higher education, all these journals are profoundly interdisciplinary).

The British Journal of Citations
Vol 1 No 1

In today's quality academic world it is increasingly important that proper recognition is made in print of the part played by one's academic colleagues in the development of one's own research. Too often such citations have to await the actual publication of research results. Now, at last, the waiting is over. *The British Journal of Citations* offers academics the chance to publish the Introductions to forthcoming research papers without the tiresome necessity of including Results or Conclusions. This means that your colleagues now have a better chance than ever of improving their ratings.
'A breakthrough' – Dr Piercemüller.

The European Journal of Negative Research Findings
Vol 1 No 1

There are inevitably times in the career of any academic when an original hypothesis is not supported by subsequent research findings. In the past this often meant that such findings went unpublished and did not therefore contribute either to personal advancement or departmental research rankings. All that has now changed. *The European Journal of Negative Research Findings* positively welcomes research papers which are unable to reach any conclusion whatsoever and which overall add precisely nothing to the total sum of human knowledge.
'Quite honestly I couldn't tell the difference between articles in here and those in other academic journals' – Maureen.

The Comparative Journal of Overnight Articles
Vol 1 No 1

Remember the times when you urgently needed an extra published article to secure promotion or nudge up your departmental research ranking? Then you need *The Comparative Journal of Overnight Articles*. No other Journal offers two editions a day and a team of independent referees from all the major disciplines on constant standby to vet your individual submission.

'If it hadn't been for The Comparative Journal *we wouldn't now be a "3" which is one grade better than Politics. Not that I believe in the system anyway'* – Professor G. Lapping.

47 The book sale

Collected University Leagues Tables ed. Geoff Hudnut and Tim Bloke.
This magnificent collection of university league tables for 1992 taken from
more than 150 sources (including the HEFC, *Sunday Times*, *The THES*, and
Exchange and Mart) allows you to find a league table in which your univer-
sity is TOPS.
'We are all in Hudnut and Bloke's debt' – Professor G. Lapping of the University of Poppleton.
(Placed first in Autocar *Top Campuses for Parking League.)*

The Last Editorials by Peter Scott.
Here in one volume are some of the best-loved editorials by the distinguished
ex-editor of *The THES*. Includes 'Whither Higher Education?' 'Whence Further Education?' and 'Was Matthew Arnold Right After All?'
'The ideal stocking filler' – Sir Peter Swinnerton-Dyer

Basic Heraldry for Sixth Form Colleges by L.E.G. Harbinger.
Now that your sixth form college has shaken off those local authority shack-
les, it's time to develop your own distinctive identity. Dr Harbinger tells you
everything you need to know about blazoning and armorial bearings – all
the way from rising phoenixes to spiralling acanthi.

Inauguration Ceremonies for Universities by G.R. Strutting.
This encyclopaedic volume tells you everything you wanted to know about
how to create an enormously long traditional inauguration ceremony for
an institution founded somewhere in the mid 1960s. Includes special chapters on 'Finding something for the local bishop to do', 'Developing a medieval prose style', and 'Stretching out the middle bit'.
'Without Strutting we'd have been hard pushed to make our ceremony last 20 minutes' – Vice
Chancellor of the City University of Poppleton.

Getting Your University Into The THES by *'A Well Known Adver-
tiser'* Make sure your university features regularly in *The Times Higher
Education Supplement*. Includes the following chapters: 'Which Rock
Star for an Honorary Degree this Year?', 'Photographs of Attractive
Women Doing Things Like Weld-
ing' and 'Long Letters Mentioning
your University at Several Points'.

Wandering in Florence by Dr R.
Piercemüller.
Once again Dr Piercemüller returns to
his beloved Tuscany. A treat for all
those who enjoyed such previous vol-
umes as *Tuscan Sabbatical* and *Research
Terms in the Chianti Hills*.
'It's always nice to discover what Dr Piercemüller
has been up to for the last year or so' – Maureen.

48 Research grant applications

Many applicants fail to understand the complex considerations which are brought to bear upon their research applications by grant awarding committees – THES

Well, gentlemen, I see it is just 10 minutes to five so perhaps we might try to find room for at least one more application before we bring matters to a close for the day. My list tells me that we must now bring our judgement to bear upon Research Application Number 8036/2/2A. This, as you see, is submitted by Doctors D. Sparking and K. Plunkett and asks for £112,000 over three years to investigate what they describe as 'the technological, social and cultural implications of the arrival of satellite television channels in the UK'. I must admit that I have no very strong feelings about this one. Indeed, I've not had a thorough chance to read the entire document in great detail. But then it is somewhat on the lengthy side.

Very lengthy, I thought , very lengthy.

Thank you, Professor Caradoc. Most helpful. Any other comments. Perhaps something on the proposed methodology?

Excuse me, Mr Chairman, but is this chap Sparking a moderately tall fellow with ginger hair?

You know him, do you, Professor Lynch?

I believe I may have come across him at last year's meeting of the BSOA, and quite frankly he didn't make too much of an impression. There was something, how might one put this, rather second-rate about his whole demeanour.

Thank you, Professor Lynch, that certainly helps to put us on the right track. Now, how about the applicants' familiarity with the existing research literature? Perhaps, Professor Turnbull, you'd like to come in on this aspect?

Certainly, Mr Chairman, I should first of all say that like yourself I have not gone into the minutiae of this proposal.

Quite so. It is *very* lengthy.

But there can be no doubt at all that Dr Plunkett, the co-researcher, is what one might call a very clever young man.

Do I detect a hint of caution there, Dr Turnbull?

You do, Mr Chairman. I think one has to say that Plunkett is also a bit too clever for his own good.

Sort of smarty-boots?

That's the type.

So, that's about it then. We seem to have covered most of the ground. And correct me if I'm wrong, but I think the consensus seems to be a straight Reject – with perhaps an invitation to resubmit?

I entirely agree, Mr Chairman. And in so doing it would obviously be helpful to the applicants if we were able to draw attention to what we consider the principal analytic deficiencies of their present proposal.

You mean we should suggest to them that what we're looking for next time is – well – how might one put it – something on the shorter side.
Exactly.

49 The new term

UNIVERSITY OF POPPLETON
Department of Media and Cultural Studies

From: Maureen
To: Professor Lapping (Head of department)
       Mr Odgers (Chairperson of board of studies)
       Dr Rawlings (New blood and safety officer)
       Dr Piercemüller (Designate library representative)
       Dr Quintock (Chairperson graduate studies)
       Ms Dibling (Student rep)
       Mr Paltry (Student rep)

As we enter the season of mists and mellow fruitfulness, I am moved to write to you with details of the forthcoming autumn term.

Student Intake

There will be 256 students in our new first year, an increase of 102 over 1993. It has not always been possible for me to accommodate those members of staff who expressed a wish not to take tutorials on Sunday evenings.

Staff-Graduate Seminars

December 9 at 8 pm (till late) Mike Tibbs (Mickey Mouse reader in hyper-reality at the City University of Bletchley) 'Why I think that on the whole New Age Travellers are in fact some sort of modern day romantics and they're not such a bad thing after all – anyway that's what I think'.

Book Lists

I'd like some.   *Contd.*

Secret Numbers

Please send me an s.a.e. to obtain your new secret numbers and passwords for the xerox machine, the stationery cupboard, the fax, and the second floor (soft-tissue) toilet facilities.

Graduate Destinations

Janet Graft, who graduated this year with a starred first, popped in to say that she may have a job on the buses.

Medical Bulletin

Dr Piercemüller phones with the news to say that he is now making good progress in the Ospedale di Verona after a severe bout of food poisoning (the zabaglione is suspected). He is grateful to all those who took the trouble to write and looks forward to thanking them each personally when he returns to the department in mid-December.

The Vice Chancellor

The Vice Chancellor will be making his unexpected visit to the department on Friday 13 November from 11.30am to 11.45am. All in all it makes one glad to be alive.

Maureen
(departmental secretary – now with added workload)

50 University league tables II

University of Poppleton
(no connection with the City of Poppleton University)

From the Office of the Vice Chancellor

Dear Colleague,
As you will know last week saw the publication of the *University League Tables* for 1994. I am delighted to tell you that the University of Poppleton achieved first place in two of these tables and a leading position in two others. Details of this splendid showing are given below

Top of the League
The University of Poppleton was placed *first* out of the United Kingdom's 96 universities in the following tables:

Universities with highest ratio of admin staff to academic tutors

1 Poppleton University	Ratio 25 to 1

Universities with highest proportion of teaching staff looking for other jobs

1 Poppleton University	99% *

* no answer received from Dr Piercemüller

Runners-Up
Despite additional competition from the so-called 'new' universities, we have successfully kept our place in the *top 10* in *two* other vital measurements of university status.

Universities with a lot of tall buildings
Average height of buildings

	Feet
1 Essex	245
2 North London	221
3 Aston	204
4 Leeds Met	196
5 Poppleton	174

Universities which are quite near the sea
Average distance to sea (in stone's throw)

	No. of throws
1 Swansea	1
2 Bangor	2
3 Aberystwyth	2.4
4 Aberdeen	3.1
5 Sunderland	4.2
6. Lancaster	6.7 *
7 Poppleton	9.5

* *This score is a weighted average based on a 'tide-in' situation*

Poll of Polls

You will be interested to learn that if these positions are added together, divided by the total number of universities, and then multiplied by the number that you first thought of, we come out nearly 20 positions ahead of the City University of Poppleton.

Yours managerially

Vice Chancellor

(voted 14th in the 1974 *Good Housekeeping Guide* to Dateable Dons)

This Week's Research Grants

Professor J.W. Cantilever, The Overseas University of Dubious Qualifications at Cambridge, £15,000 from the Astrology Research Council for a study of the recent way in which Aries subjects have had their romantic plans affected by the Moon opposing Pluto in Scorpio.

51 The student charter

UNIVERSITY OF POPPLETON
from the office of the Vice Chancellor

The Student Charter

I enclose the terms of the Student Charter as agreed by the Student Charter Sub-Committee (myself as chairman, Professors Dobbins, Evans, Lapping, Porterhouse, Stibling as full members, and an ex-officio student representative who because of vacation was unable to attend the final meeting).

This Charter sets out the rights and responsibilities of students (or 'customers') and the University of Poppleton towards each in the teaching/learning relationship.

Article One. All students have the inalienable right to expect academic lectures to take place at the stated time and in the stated place subject to the following exemptions:
(a) Lectures which start and finish early
(b) Lectures given by elderly or disorientated members of staff
(c) Lectures cancelled because of illness or weather conditions

Article Two. All students have the inalienable right to expect that their lectures and seminars will take place in *rooms* which provide adequate space for discussions and note-taking.
(a)The word 'room' in this context is taken to include: Exhibition and gallery areas, corridors, bike sheds, and that little spot in B block behind the ventilation shaft.
(b)The phrase 'adequate space' in this context is based on objective evidence that sufficient air is available at all times for *regular* but not *deep* breathing.

Article Three. All students have the inalienable right to expect that their essays will be marked and returned within *eight weeks* subject to the following exceptions:
(a) Longish essays

(b) Essays handed in at awkward times

Article Four. All students have the inalienable right to expect that their marked essays will display the following clear evidence of assessment:
(a) A few ticks here and there

(b) A brief indication that the work could have been better

Compensation.
If any of these articles are violated then affected students will be entitled to compensation in the form of one voucher for each violation. This may be exchanged at the end of the final year for a B+ essay mark in a course of their choice.

nb. The above compensation scheme does not apply on any of the academic routes at present served by Dr Piercemüller.

52 The after dinner speech

'And now it gives me great pleasure to introduce our after dinner speaker. Professor Lapping is Professor of Media and Culture at the University of Poppleton which is of course a next door neighbour to our Poppleton branch of *WindowGlaze*. He's come here tonight to talk about "The Role of Double Glazing in the Postmodern World". Ladies and Gentlemen. Professor Topping.'

'Ladies and Gentlemen, Managing Director of *WindowGlaze*.'

(tells old joke which is poorly received)

'It gives me great pleasure to stand here tonight in that for many years I have advocated closer links between the academic and the business community. I fervently believe we have a lot to teach each other.'

(sounds of ribaldry from a table near the back)

'In a way I regard tonight as "a window of opportunity" – even "a double-glazed window of opportunity" – to talk about how your concerns of the postmodern world very much mesh with my own'.

(two or three bread rolls are thrown across the room)

'You see, in many ways, our postmodern culture is quintessentially a culture of visibility. Never before has there been so much emphasis on the "look". And much of this "looking" is now done through glass. We look through glass at the flickering images of television, we look through the glass from behind the wheel of our car, and we look through glass every time we sit down at our word processor.'

(the room looks suddenly emptier)

'But this sense of "looking through", this search for that which lies behind the glass, this desire to appropriate the mediated image, is nowhere more evident than when we look through a window, when we – and how appropriate the phrase is – when we "window-glaze".'

(audible groans)

'But there is more to the parallel than that. For in this hyperreal Baudrillardian culture of spectacle, there is a sense in which the visible is "invisible", a sense in which the image excludes the reality which it previously represented'.

(sounds of laughter from the bar outside)

'How true that is of "double glazing" where *your* excellent windows, whatever their transom and mullion effect, whether Queen Anne, Elizabethan or Georgian, simultaneously open on to the world and close it off. As your slogan so eloquently puts it "Double glazing keeps the outside out and the inside in". What better way could there be of conceptualising the paradox of the visible in the postmodern world?'

(waiters start stacking chairs)

'Thank you for inviting me and, in conclusion, may I wish every one of you good luck and top sales in the coming year.'

(there is no one left to receive the wish)

53 The university newsletter

The development of ... unread newsletters ... seems to be a major part of the job description for today's higher education administrator – THES

Closed Circuit
The University of Poppleton's Very Own Newsletter

A Letter from the Vice Chancellor

I'm delighted to have this opportunity of writing again for *Closed Circuit*. When I first took this post. Not so much a university as a community. Difficult but exciting times. Everyone can contribute. The next millennium.

Yours sincerely

The Vice Chancellor

New Appointments

A big Poppleton 'Hello' to the following

Andrew Timmins (BA Manchester) (PhD Leicester) who has been appointed temporary lecturer in First Year Seminars in the Department of English. Welcome, Andy.

And it's time to say goodbye and good luck for the future to the following members of staff who bid farewell last term: Lionel Grout (BA Manchester) (PhD Nottingham) who has taken early retirement from his position as temporary lecturer in First Year Seminars in the Department of English because of 'incremental drift'. Nice to have known you, Lionel.

DON'T FORGET THIS IS YOUR PAPER AND WE'D LOVE TO HEAR YOUR VIEWS ON ANYTHING AND EVERYTHING

Letters to the Editor

Dear Sir

May I say how much I like the new Closed Circuit.

Congratulations to all concerned

G.K. Dobbin (Senior Administrative Officer)

THANKS A MILLION FOR YOUR LETTER, GEOFF. AND NOW IT'S YOUR TURN, WHY NOT SIT DOWN NOW AND GET THAT BOUQUET (OR BRICKBAT!) OFF *YOUR* CHEST. KEEP THOSE LETTERS ROLLING IN!

Departmental News

Department of Biology

Two people in the department have given papers to badly attended seminars at other universities. Someone has been invited to a conference in Holland.

Department of Mathematics

One member of staff appeared briefly on local radio.

For sale

Small, damp, uninviting basement flat somewhere on the outskirts of Poppleton. Try any offer. Apply L. Grout, c/o Dept. English

In our next issue Professor D.W.D. Dugdale goes 'Down Your Way' round our planned Science Park.

So that's agreed. the department will pay for the external examiner's wine irrespective of actual consumption, but if, he also orders a large Glenfiddich, then the cost will be subtracted from his overnight allowance. Excellent. May we now turn to Item 29? We are invited by the HEFC to provide a 10-page assessment of our departmental quality.

Why don't we just say that we're absolutely bloody marvellous?

As usual, Mr Odgers, you've come straight to the point. The problem is, however, that if we do say our teaching is 'absolutely bloody marvellous' or to use the recommended term, 'excellent', then the council may not believe us and send inspectors in to check.

And if they find we're lying?

Then we could be declared 'satisfactory' or even 'unsatisfactory'.

So it's best to say we're 'satisfactory'.

There is that school of opinion. But there's also the view that so many departments will put themselves down as 'excellent' that there won't be time for the inspectors to visit every one. That means there's a fair chance of being declared 'excellent' without inspection.

So you're saying we should describe ourselves as 'excellent'?

Yes, but perhaps not as too excellent in that there is also the view that those departments which describe themselves uncritically as 'excellent' are the most likely 'excellent' department to be visited. It might therefore be wiser to say 'excellent' and then add a couple of minor reservations.

Won't that mean that they'll simply look at those reservations and say this department looks more like 'satisfactory' than 'excellent'?

That's always possible, but that's a far better result than describing ourselves as 'satisfactory' with reservations and then getting knocked back to 'unsatisfactory'.

So you advise going for 'excellent' with reservations?

I do.

I've got an idea. What about describing ourselves as 'unsatisfactory' on the grounds that no-one else will do that and therefore we'll stand out as exceptionally honest and therefore be considered for an 'excellent'?

I'm sorry, Dr Quintock. You're now being rather silly.

.

55 Top-up fees

Good evening and welcome to It's Principles That Count, the hard-hitting show in which top decision-makers discuss the fundamental principles behind key issues of the day. This week we're debating the controversial LSE proposal that undergraduate students should be charged top-up fees of £500 a year. And in the hot-seat we have a representative of the CVCP, who at his own request will only be appearing in silhouette. Good evening, Vice Chancellor 'X'.

Good evening, Jeremy.

Vice Chancellor 'X', would it not be true to say that the CVCP has been opposed to tuition fees on the traditional principle that higher education should be free?

You could say that.

And also on the egalitarian principle that there should be the same opportunity for all students with appropriate entrance qualifications to enter higher education?

That's more or less correct.

And also no doubt on the democratic principle that higher education should remain a single system and not one invidiously divided between universities which can attract fee-paying students and those that can't?

One could go as far as that.

And perhaps also on the political principle that universities should stick together and find collective ways to resist the Government's cuts in tuition fees?

That might come into it.

In view of all those principles might we not have expected a statement from the CVCP condemning the LSE move?

I think what we're faced with here is a contradiction between those principles and an important new principle which deserves consideration.

Which principle is that exactly?

The important new principle that as long as you can find someone else to do your dirty work for you, then there's no need for you to show your head above the parapet.

Unless it's a silhouette?

Exactly.

Thank you, Vice Chancellor 'X'. Admirably clear. One could hardly imagine the minister himself putting it more coherently

Thank you.

Thank you and goodnight. Next week on this show, we'll be looking at the basic principles behind the cuts in the invalidity benefit. Till then, goodbye. And remember. It's Principles That Count.

56 Expanding student numbers

'Institutions should be completely honest in their prospectuses about the size of their lectures and classes' – article on the expansion in student numbers – THES

Introducing Cultural Studies.

A One Term First Year Course by Professor Gordon Lapping.

All lectures on this course are held in Rumbelows Lecture Theatre (formerly Polly Peck Lecture Theatre). Seating capacity *(including gangway steps, top of the radiators and epidiascope trolley)* 250.

For lectures One to Four the average composition and size of the audience for this lecture course as monitored by the Central Statistical Bureau (Mr A. J. Wormald) is as follows:

175 first year students from the Department of Cultural and Media Studies.

45 first year students from the Psychology Department who invariably seize on this optional chance to avoid Professor Redknap's distinctly unethical introductory course on *Sticking Electrodes into Chicken's Brains*.

12 mature students on the much heralded Open Access course who, having received no proper advice whatsoever on what they should be doing, simply drift into the first lecture they come across. Two elderly gentlemen with cans of Carlsberg Special.

Mr 'X' – a freelance infiltrator.

Half-a-dozen film buffs left over from the previous night's screening by the Film Society of Ingmar Bergman's *Cries and Whispers*.

Four accredited appraisers with clipboards.

Two senior appraisers with larger clipboards appraising the accredited appraisers.

12 trainee appraisers 'observing' both sets of appraisers.

Professor Lapping's elderly mother, Winifred Mary Lapping, who often finds herself 'at something of a loose end' on a Thursday morning.

20 to 30 overseas students who are already beginning to suspect that this is all they are going to get for their money.

The increasingly beleaguered Vice Chancellor in a clumsy disguise.

Professor Gordon Lapping.

Statistically Computed Mean Total: 285.

For lectures Five to Nine, the average composition and size of the audience for this lecture course as monitored by the Central Statistical Bureau (Mr A. J. Wormald) is as follows:

Seven or eight first year students.

Professor Lapping's mother.

Professor Lapping (substituted after 45 minutes).

Statistically Computed Mean Total: A good handful.

(n.b. there is no lecture on this course in the first week of term 'in order to allow the new students to find their way around' and the lectures in weeks four and seven are traditionally cancelled to allow students and staff to attend their respective Days of Action.)

57 The *THES* problem page

According to The Daily Telegraph diary on 11 April 1991, one of the top contenders on the short list of possible new titles for the Times Higher Education Supplement *is* Forum *– the name of the popular magazine devoted to sexual problems*

LETTERS TO THE EDITOR

Sir, – I keep waking up at night worrying about the length of my curriculum vitae. I always thought it was more substantial than anyone else's in the department but when I took it out and showed it to my head of department at a recent meeting to discuss possible promotion, he told me that 'quite frankly' it was not long enough to be 'effective'. What do you advise?

Yours faithfully,

(name and address supplied).

(Nurse Linda Lovejoy replies: *Why not try some of the well-known cv extension techniques: pretend that a couple of journal reviews are really articles; put down second editions and translations of books as new publications; describe the book that you are at present working on as 'in press'. It's a sad fact but no longer will anyone take the quality of your cv into account. In today's academic world size really does matter.*)

Sir, – I was fascinated to read your recent article on 'Academic dress throughout the ages'. I myself have always regarded degree day as the highlight of the university year. As far as I'm concerned there's no bigger thrill than being in the Ede and Ravenscroft robing room immediately before the ceremony and watching all those professors and rectors and provosts standing in front of the full-length mirror adjusting their multi-coloured gowns and hoods. Some of those gowns are really silky! And one year we had an American visitor whose gown actually zipped up in front. But for my money there's nothing to beat that furry bit on the Leicester PhD. Wow! That one really takes the proverbial mace. Have any of your readers similar robing room stories?

Yours faithfully,

(name and address supplied).

Sir, – I wonder if you can help me. I'm a happily married 45-year-old man at present employed as a lecturer in a respected university department. According to my head of department I am extremely likely to be promoted to senior lecturer in the very near future. My problem is this: in the last few years I've found myself simply longing to dress in women's clothes. Quite frankly, I would like nothing more than to turn up for work tomorrow wearing a dress or a skirt. What do you advise?

Yours faithfully,

(name and address supplied).

(Nurse Linda Lovejoy says: *Under no circumstances whatsoever must you turn up to work at a British university looking like a woman. All the available statistical evidence suggests that this would seriously jeopardise your promotion prospects.*)

58 The staff questionnaire

A survey at Southampton University has revealed that some academic staff were incapable of answering straight questions – THES

UNIVERSITY OF POPPLETON
CAR PARKING QUESTIONNAIRE (1993/6/778/C)

Please answer all questions by ticking your preferred answer.

Do you have a car? Yes ❑ No ❑
If you mean do I own a car then technically the answer is 'No', in that my wife and I are co-owners of a car. If, however, you are asking whether or not I drive a car (without any implications of ownership) then the answer is 'Yes'.

Do you regularly drive your car into work? Yes ❑ No ❑
If you are asking if I drive my car in an habitual, steady, uniform, manner which could be said to conform to established driving practice rather than in an irregular, eccentric fashion (for example, by engaging third gear, immediately after selecting first or by indicating 'right' when turning 'left') then I would say 'Yes'. If, however, your reference is not to the regularity of my mode of driving but to my tendency to drive my car at 'regular' intervals of time, then my answer would obviously depend on what you mean by 'regular', upon how 'regular' is 'regular'. I wouldn't, therefore, at this stage of the questionnaire, like to commit myself one way or the other.

Thinking about parking over the last year, how would you describe your own experience of car parking arrangements at the university: Satisfactory Fairly Satisfactory Unsatisfactory.
I'm afraid that your grammatically unsatisfactory formulation poses an impossible phenomenological task. In common I suspect with others among your respondents I have certainly not been 'thinking about parking over the last year', and I am not therefore able to cast myself into such a remembered frame of mind in order to proceed to the second experimental part of your question.

Taking everything into account, would you say that on the whole it was fair and reasonable that senior members of the administrative staff should have reserved parking spaces on campus? Yes ❑ No ☑

Now please turn over
If this is to be read as an acrobatic injunction then I am inclined to disobey, if however ...

Say good bye to long walks from car to office and lecture hall

The University of Poppleton is proud to announce its brand new

BUSINESS CLASS PARKING SCHEME.

For only £1000 per annum you may purchase your very own space in one of the parking zones formerly reserved for the most senior members of the university. Choose from one of the following yellow painted logos:

HEAD OF THE APPEAL FUND

VICE-CHANCELLOR

CVCP AUDIT COMMITTEE ONLY

59 The external examiner

'Universities are having an external examiners' crisis as academies are increasingly unwilling to take on this onerous and low-paid work' – THES

You're through to Professor Astle.

Thank you, Maureen. Geoffrey, is that really you? Gordon here. Gordon Lapping. Good to speak to you. Long time no see, eh? How are you? And the lovely Elizabeth?

Patricia. Elizabeth was the first Mrs Astle.

Of course she was. Of course she was. *Tempus fugit*, Geoffrey. Ask not for whom etcetera.

Was there anything specific?

Specific?

Any *specific* reason for this call?

Not really, Geoffrey. Not really. Just wanted to say hello and chew over the old fat and sort of ask if by any chance you were free on 24 June this year.

24 June?

That's right. We'd rather like to invite you over to Poppleton for a little staff dinner. A couple of laughs. A few drinks. You know the sort of thing. Two star B and B. A cheque in the back pocket for £200 and a lift to and from the station in Dr Quintock's Rover.

Well, I ...

And in return if you could possibly see your way clear to glance over a bijou bundle of our final scripts. You know the sort of thing. Randomly raise and lower a few marginals. Show a bit of liberality on the aegrotats. And then more or less normal distribution and Bob's your uncle. One 'pass'. Two or three 'thirds'. And most of the rest 'lowers' or 'uppers' with just enough 'firsts' left over to give us the edge on Politics who have their Exam Board the day before. What do you say?

No more than 20 scripts through the post?

Top whack.

No seat next to Mr Odgers at the dinner?

Guaranteed.

No joint boards?

No joint boards.

It's good to do business with you, Gordon.

And you, Geoffrey.

Forward to higher standards.

What else?

60 PhD theses

British library plans to market PhD theses commercially – THES

English Literature

Witchcraft Images in Shakespearean Tragedy.

Dr Finola Skimshanks spent eight years on this computer analysis of 'witchcraft images' in three Shakespearean tragedies (*Hamlet, Macbeth* and *Othello*). She firmly establishes that there are significantly more references to witches and their practices in *Macbeth* ($p > 0.05$) than in either of the other plays, and in a virtually incomprehensible penultimate chapter offers no explanation whatsoever for her findings.

£205.40

Political Science

The Marxian Meta-Narrative: Congruities and Convergences in Post-Modernist Thought.

In this fascinating ESRC thesis, Dr Vic Tumbril, attempts with mounting desperation to reconcile the contemporary post-modernist arguments of Michel Foucault, Jacques Derrida, Jean-Francois Lyotard, Uncle Tom Cobleigh, Paul de Man and Gilles Deleuze, with the totally unsubstantiated but amiably nostalgic view that the British working class is about to become the revolutionary instrument of social change.

£125.60 (*n.b. A section from Chapter Eight entitled 'What To Do Now' is available in pamphlet form at 25p*).

Psychology

Emotional Variables in the Short-Term Recall of Nonsense Syllables.

After five introductory chapters in which the author, Dr Trevor Dewlap, paraphrases every known research paper on the subject since the year dot, we at last reach the flimsy middle section in which thirty students with nothing else to do on a Wednesday afternoon show that they are rather better at the short-term recall of nonsense syllables when sitting around smoking in the laboratory than when isolated in cubicles and 'emotionally aroused' by the delivery of electrical shocks to their ear-lobes. In his conclusion, Dr Dewlap turns to the policy implications of all this but can't think of any.

£250 (*please add £10 for pull-out list of nonsense syllables*).

Social Work and Social Policy

The Social Origins of Part-Time Youth Club Workers

Dr Cressida Tudor-Peak reveals that part-time youth club leaders are 'on the middle-class side of things' compared to the clubs' attendees. In a challenging final chapter she argues that more research is needed in order to establish whether the best solution to this disjunction might be widening the social class recruitment base for part-time youth club leaders, or the 'more radical option' of banning the working class from youth clubs altogether.

£15 (*special six-pack edition designed for youth club leaders – £75*).

History

The Iconography of Late Medieval Portuguese Mortuary Practices: a Study of Portraits and Portraiture (1502 – 1578)

In this refreshing thesis, Dr Thomas Gangling (formerly of Utrecht University) establishes that in the period under review there was a dramatic increase in the average number of people portrayed in Portuguese mourning portraits. In a challenging, though syntactically shoddy, final chapter, he argues that may: 1) reflect an increase in family size; 2) the desire of complete strangers to have their portraits painted; 3) the possibility that the medieval Portuguese were having two to three groups of mourners painted simultaneously.

£150 (o.n.o).

61 The CVCP

Twenty-three new 'Vice Chancellors' will be attending the next meeting of the CVCP – THES

Charles, would you mind awfully saying a few welcoming words to these new chappies.

What sort of thing did you have in mind, Gerald?

Something pretty general along the lines of Welcome to the Committee. Strength in numbers. Delighted they're able to join us.

I wonder if 'delighted' sounds a trifle gushing?

You were thinking more along the lines of 'fairly pleased'?

Exactly.

That would be perfectly adequate. And then perhaps a few words about our progressive policy orientation over the past few years. The strategic manner in which we've fought against some of the more irrational government policies by more or less ...

Going along with them.

That's the type of thing. And then perhaps you could slip in something about dress.

Dress?

Some casual reference to the fact that on the whole, for reasons of tradition, we prefer to attend committee meetings in suits.

Does that need saying? One would have thought ...

Quite so. But it appears that one or two of their number positively favour plumbers' trousers.

You mean jeans?

That's right. And if you have time, perhaps a cautionary word about the display of ostentatious jewellery.

Jewellery?

One understands that at least one of our new chappies wears a ring.

That's hardly 'ostentatious'.

Through the ear?

I see what you mean.

And then it's more or less plain sailing. Don't mention the Athenaeum or they'll all be applying, pop in a word about the port being passed to the left and that the usual rule for the cutlery is to work inwards.

And that's it?

I think so. I suggest you pause at that point, announce that lunch is served, and then Antonia will come in and show them all to the kitchens.

62 Promotion

And now may we turn to Item Six: 'Promotions to Senior Lecturer'. You will recall from our last meeting that there were originally 472 lecturers submitted in this category but that the Finance Committee recommended only one such promotion this year. We therefore whittled down the numbers to the two names you see before you: Dr Adams of Physics and Dr Lipchitz of Chemistry. Perhaps we might start by considering their research claims. Professor Dunton, I believe you have the figures.

Yes indeed, Vice Chancellor. Adam has written 12 major books, whereas Lipchitz can boast 13. But Lipchitz has only 145 published articles compared to Adams' total of 157 – although three of the latter were co-authored.

Which rather suggests that Adams may be lacking in independent thought.

Or that he's rather more sociable than Lipchitz.

Indeed. Might we move on to reports from external referees. Professor Germayne, I believe you have these to hand.

That's right Vice Chancellor. Adams' referee, an internationally respected physicist, writes to say that 'Overall, Dr Adams is simply the best: an unquestionably stupendous researcher, an indubitably magnificent teacher, and a first-class administrator'.

'First-class' sounds a trifle grudging.

I thought so too.

Compared to 'stupendous' and 'magnificent' it has a dying fall.

Quite so.

And the reference for Lipchitz?

This is from an internationally respected chemist. It concludes: 'Lipchitz leads the field: he is an absolutely outstanding researcher, an utterly superb teacher and an incomparable administrator'.

'Incomparable' is somewhat ambiguous. One might be incomparable because one was incomparably bad.

Indeed.

So if we rule out 'first-class' and 'incomparable', we find that Adams is nothing much more than 'stupendous' and 'magnificent' while Lipchitz is merely 'outstanding' and 'superb'. In the circumstances there seems only one way to resolve the problem.

Vice Chancellor?

I suggest we make no promotion to senior lecturer this year on the grounds that in today's competitive climate neither candidate reached an acceptable level of excellence.

Hear, hear.

And now may we turn to Item Seven: Proposals to subtract performance related pay from existing staff. Do we have a seconder?

63 Staff development

The Senior Staff Development Officer will see you now, Dr Piercemüller.

Thank you.

Ah, Piercemüller. So, that's what you look like.

I'm sorry I wasn't able to pop over as planned last term but things have rather tended to pile up. And then there's been the old back.

The back?

Spasms. No real alternative but to lie down immediately.

Well, I'm sorry about your problems, Dr Piercemüller, but we have to face the unfortunate truth that since your appointment at this university nearly twenty-three years ago you have never attended a training workshop, visited any of the eleven exhibitions of educational technology held on campus, or taken advantage of a single one of the sixty-three widely advertised sessions on staff development organised by myself and my specialist team of highly trained staff developers.

What with one thing and another.

Dr Piercemüller, how do you manage in the teaching situation.

The teaching situation?

Do you employ video aids? An OHP for example?

Not exactly, no.

An epidiascope? Flip charts? Large Screen Computer Projection? Automatic Response Systems?

Not as such.

And have you thought about problem based learning? Or fieldwork? Or team teaching? Or resource based learning? Or syndicate groups?

Only now and then.

So how do you manage in the teaching situation?

The teaching situation? Well, I stand up and more or less read out the notes for an hour and then more or less stop.

Dr Piercemüller, I want to ask you a very serious question. Have you ever considered the effects of this type of teaching practice? The total boredom? The complete lack of stimulation? The mind-numbing predictability?

It's very nice of you to ask. But on the whole ...

Yes.

I find that if I have a stiff gin before I start it's not too bad at all.

64 Dealing with freshers

At this very moment thousands of people are busily preparing themselves for their first days in Britain's institutions of higher education. As a special service to these 'freshers', *The THES* has recruited Professor 'L', a senior academic at one of the country's leading middle-rank universities, to answer some of the queries which have recently been tumbling through our mailbox.

Q. Louise (Carshalton): *I'm due to take up a place at the University of Tewkesbury this October but friends tell me there is no such university. What do you advise?*

Professor 'L' writes: **I have to say it's a new one on me. But then again I may have missed something in the press. Don't start worrying yet. These are early days in higher education. Tewkesbury could well make it by early October.**

Q. Darren (Tewkesbury): *I will be going up to read History at Southampton this October. Is there any preparatory work you could recommend?*

Professor 'L': **Try working on your vocabulary. Nobody 'goes up' or 'reads' at Southampton. And why travel so far? What's the matter with your local university?**

Q. Michelle (Banbury): *I've been accepted at a Northern university this October but I'm a very nervous and unattractive person and worry that I won't be able to make any friends. Can you help?*

Professor 'L': **Put such worries right out of your mind. Nearly all universities now supply a number of evangelical Christians in each residential block. Quite frankly, they'll speak to any one.**

Q. Zak (Highgate): *My father tells me that a great deal of my time in higher education will be spent in intimate tutorials with top professors. Have you any tips on how to speak to such eminent people?*

Professor 'L': **Where's your father been for the past decade? Underground? As a first year you will be taught solely by people with cheap clothes and harrowed expressions who are three years older than yourself. Try to be nice to them. Nobody else wants the work.**

Q. 'Bunty' (Carlisle): *I'm off to the University of Poppleton in just three weeks' time to study cultural studies. It's a completely new subject for me and I keep wondering if I will fit in.*

Professor 'L': **Having checked over the seminar and lecture numbers in the department of your choice and noted your nick-name, I have to say I doubt it.**

This Week's Research Grants

Professor J.W. Toadie, University of Blanding,£327,000 from the Home Office for an in-depth investigation which will either establish the extraordinarily beneficial effects of current Government policies on law-and-order or never see the light of day. (Extension of previous grant.)

THIS WEEK'S SICK NOTES

Student Notice Board

To All Students

Dr Piercemüller very much regrets that he will not be available to give a single one of his time-tabled lectures or seminars this week or next because he is definitely going down with one of those bugs which simply lay you out and make you feel absolutely unable to do anything very much but sit in a warm room at home with a mug of Bovril and watch hour after hour of daytime television.

Students should go on with whatever work they are doing.

Ken Livingstone Hall of Residence
Tuesday

Dear Professor Lapping

I'm sorry that I will not be able to come to your 9.15 am seminar on Post Modernism this Thursday even though I was supposed to give the paper at the seminar but I have been sick with this very nasty virus which has been going round and I will not be well tomorrow or the day after that which is Thursday come to that.

Yours sincerely

(First year, Red hair, From Bristol)

DEPARTMENT OF MEDIA AND CULTURAL STUDIES

URGENT NOTICE: SICK NOTES

Please note that there is no-one in the departmental office until further notice to receive sick notes from students because of sickness.

All sick notes should therefore be handed to the appropriate tutor in person.

If the tutor is sick then the note should be retained until such time as the tutor recovers from such sickness or lack of sickness allows this office to re-open.

I hope this is clear.

pp. Maureen

UNIVERSITY OF POPPLETON HEALTH CENTRE

Dear Student

The University Health Centre very much regrets that it will not be possible for Dr T.W.F. Carstairs to issue any more medical certificates to students as from noon today (Monday).

Dr Carstairs went home shortly after coffee break this morning with itchy eyes, tickly throat, and a very nasty sort of yucky feeling behind his nose.

pp. T.W.F. Carstairs

91

66 Equal opportunities

Maureen.

Professor Lapping?
Doing anything particular at this precise moment?

No, nothing particular. I was just generally sorting over 600 continuous assessment essays into subject areas and then generally distributing them into fourteen marking pairs and then generally collating course marks in preparation for the examiners meeting.

Because I was wondering if you knew anything about all this stuff in my pigeon hole.

The long letter I sent to the Vice Chancellor on Quality Control or the eight-page questionnaire I completed on Quality Audit for the HEQC?

Neither of those.

My five-page summary of the department's views on Quality Assessment for the FEFCE?

No, this is something different. Some stuff about 95 per cent of university professors being men.

Who'd have thought it?

And then there's a long list of figures from universities all round the country showing that male academics are far more likely to be recommended for merit awards than women.

Almost unbelievable.

And an article with a graph showing that women are more frequently appointed at the bottom of academic pay scales and that the average weekly earnings of male teachers in higher and further education is £440.90 whereas women only earn £373.50.

Whatever next?

And then a long piece attacking universities for failing to set targets to improve the situation and for a complete lack of interest in monitoring progress in the area.

You'd like me to put it on the agenda for the next departmental meeting?

Not just yet, Maureen. Not while we're up to our eyes in Quality business.

A question of priorities?

Exactly. Still, thank goodness there's a bright side to all this stuff.

There is?

All in all, Maureen, it must make you glad you're not an academic.

One counts one's blessings, Professor Lapping.

67 The university inauguration

The Inauguration Ceremony of the City University of Poppleton
(formerly Poppleton Polytechnic)

to be held in
+ Poppleton Cathedral +
in the presence of

The Bishop of Poppleton
Mr G.D.R. Loneshark (Governor)
Mr Wayne Pillock (Captain Poppleton Town F.C.)
Dr F.B. Ranting (Headmaster of Saint Optouts School, Poppleton)
Brigadier L.C. Clusterbomb (Poppleton OTC)
P.K. Stairwell (Chief Constable, Poppleton and District)
Assorted macebearers
Lots of new professors
Two students with reasonable suits

ORDER OF CEREMONY

1 Welcome by the Bishop of Poppleton
On behalf of the Cathedral of Poppleton, the Board of Governors, Loneshark Plc, and
God Almighty, I welcome you here today to inaugurate the City University of
Poppleton.
Congregation reply: And welcome to you, Oh Bishop.

2 Proclamation (read by a man up for the day from the Privy Council)
I hereby declare that Her Majesty's Privy Council has consented that Poppleton Polytechnic shall henceforth be known as The City University of Poppleton and shall be treated for all purposes as a university.
Congregation reply: *Thanks a lot, Oh Privy Council.*

3 The Chancellor is Installed
Whereas the Board of Governors did resolve to appoint a Chancellor and did spend two or three months looking round without much success but eventually resolved to appoint an aristocratic buffoon, I hereby invite that buffoon to step forward for installation as Chancellor.
Congregation reply: *We welcome you to our new university. May things go well with you. Welcome.*

4 The Chancellor Responds
Thank you for your welcome. Let this university now go forward on its mission. And thanks again for the welcome.
Congregation reply: *Don't mention it.*

5 Ceremonial Waving of Paper Napkins
At this moment all members of the congregation rise and wave complimentary paper napkins in the air to symbolise the granting of degrees by the new university.

6 Exeunt Omnes
Processions leave the cathedral singing the City University of Poppleton's new specially composed hymn 'May Our Mission Never Drift'
Congregation reply (in a mutter): *All in all it makes you wonder who picked up the tab for this little lot.*

68 Quality I

'Universities have many systems for checking the quality of institutions and courses but they are not addressing at individual level how good the teaching is. They are terrified of making it personal'
– Cari Loder, of The Centre for Higher Education Studies.

The Teaching Assessment Committee will see you now, Dr Ronaldson.

Thank you.

Ah, Ronaldson. Do take a seat. As I understand it, you have been before this committee on a previous occasion.

Yes, Vice Chancellor. You withheld an increment from me last term as a penalty for my failure to use the slide projector in circumstances where it was considered appropriate.

That was during your second year course on ethics.

Indeed.

Well, Ronaldson, there are now other matters to which this committee must turn its attention. For a start, there's your continued failure to issue this committee with a set of goals for your epistemology course – a set of goals which could be matched against student performance.

I explained last time that my general goal was to raise doubts about standard ways of 'knowing'.

But, Ronaldson, that's only one goal. And a general one at that. As you know perfectly well, this committee insists upon a minimum of six specific goals per course. Anything less is seen as stinting.

I'm sorry.

And no doubt you're equally sorry about your incapacity to lecture in a comprehensible manner. According to the latest student questionnaire, 22 per cent say that you 'have a tendency to make contradictory statements'.

As high as that?

And 41 per cent agree with the statement that you are 'inclined to make matters more complicated than they need to be'. That's nearly half, Ronaldson. Nearly half.

It is indeed.

Let me be quite frank. We've been generous with you in the past. We've overlooked your incapacity to issue book lists of sufficient length, your occasional failure to lecture for the full 60 minutes and your languid demeanour at the lectern. But I have to say that unless there is an immediate overall improvement in your teaching we may have to entertain the possibility of dismissal. Now, could I be clearer than that, Dr Ronaldson?

Not without slides, Vice Chancellor.

69 The new universities

YOUR QUESTIONS ANSWERED
This week: the new universities

Dear Sir

Which of the new universities has the longest name?

There are those who insist that the winner is the University of Glamorgan (Prifysgol Morgannwg) (Pontypridd) with a grand total of 49 letters and two sets of brackets. But as part of that name is a translation of the other part, then the true winner is the University of Central England in Birmingham (Perry Barr) with 47 letters and one set of brackets.

Dear Sir

I've been accepted for Staffordshire University and was due to start there this week but so far, despite a great deal of travelling around, I've not been able to trace it. It certainly doesn't seem to be in Stafford or Newcastle-un-der-Lyme.

Don't worry. You've been very close. In fact Staffordshire University is in Stoke-on-Trent. Just on the right as you come down the High Street.

Dear Sir

I'm at the University of Central Lancashire in Preston but when I look at the map Preston is nowhere near the centre of Lancashire. It's right over to one side.

Don't be so pedantic.

Dear Sir

I believe that I may be a student at the only British university with a name which contains a comma – 'University of the West of England, Bristol'?

It's difficult to tell from your letter whether you are boasting or complaining. But you are right in your belief. Most other new universities prefer brackets but one – Glasgow Polytechnic/The Queens College – has, as you can see for yourself, an oblique. In casual conversation such punctuation differences need not be marked.

Dear Sir

I am a student at the University of Northumbria at Newcastle whereas my friend attends the new University of Central England in Birmingham. We wonder if any significance should be attached to this prepositional difference?

It is generally agreed that to describe a university as at a place rather than in it suggests a degree of greater accidentality. So the University of Northumbria at Newcastle could arguably be somewhere else other than Newcastle, whereas the University of Central England in Birmingham implies that the Birmingham location was virtually unavoidable.

70 Office space

University of Poppleton
Department of Space Management

Dear Professor Lapping,

I am pleased to tell you that the re-calculation of the PSRs (Person-Space Ratios) for your department is now complete. As you will recall this new ratio now takes into account not only the space inside your room but also an area of approximately two square feet outside your door (the so-called Porch Space) and the unused area between your head and the ceiling of your room (an Altitude Area of approximately 14 square feet)

1. Your Present Office Under Existing PSR Ratios

2. Your Office after PSR re-calculation

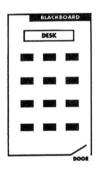

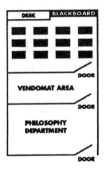

As you will see from the above the new PSR involves the insertion of a simple bi-secting divider which will enable the former back third of your office to be converted into new premises for the Philosophy Department, and the insertion of a smaller divider at the back of your new office to create a Vendomat area as a replacement for the existing SCR facilities. Your blackboard has been reduced by one half to accommodate this change (smaller writing is recommended).

Your own personal desk has been replaced by a smaller model which fea-

tures a front opening lid action and a socket for inkwell. Our committee recommends that you avoid extravagant gestures during teaching and reduce the amount of fatty food in your present diet.

Yours in space

D.J. Curtailing
(Assistant Director)

APPOINTMENTS
UNIVERSITY OF
POPPLETON

UNIVERSITY DISCRIMINATION
OFFICER
c.£50,000
As Discrimination Officer you will
be required to ensure that the Real
University of Poppleton is clearly
discriminated from the upstart 'City
University of Poppleton'. This
involves daily scrutiny of press,
radio, and television for misleading
references and the subsequent
dispatch of legal writs. You will
work directly to the Real Vice
Chancellor of the University of
Poppleton who is pig sick about the
whole business.

71 The university video II

University video-cassette committee

Minutes of meeting held on 28 February

Present:
Professor K.R. Moresby
Professor L.P.W. Stanstead
Dr T.W.P. Lutin
Dr O.P. Mendip
Dr M.K. Stormporch
Dr S.T. Turpitz (chairman)
Mr Wayne Purfleet (student)

Apologies for Absence:
The Vice Chancellor
Dr R.S. Tantaliser
Mr L.S. Portly

45/94 Matters Arising

With reference to 126/93, it was reported by Mr Wayne Purfleet (in attendance only) that the university 'band' which the present committee had invited to provide the musical accompaniment for the proposed university video had now changed its name from *Heartbeats of Desire* to *Mucous Membrane*. After reassurances from the student representatives that the 'sound' made by this group was, for all intents and purposes, indistinguishable from that made by the previous one, it was agreed to confirm the invitation.

46/94 Professor Chillingbeck's Vowel Sounds

Dr Lutin (co-director of university video) reported to the committee on his conversation with Professor Chillingbeck of the linguistics department. It had been carefully explained to Professor Chillingbeck that the original section of the university video devoted to the work of his department had been thought by the committee to 'lack visual impact', and his own contribution – a virtuoso recital of the principal Yoruba vowel sounds – while admirably oriented to Third World concerns, might, when viewed out of context, appear mildly ridiculous. The committee thanked Dr Lutin for his report and agreed to the total exclusion of the linguistics department from the university video.

47/94 Vice Chancellor's refusal to Sit on Desk

Professor Moresby (key grip) reported that a new desk had now been obtained following the Vice Chancellor's refusal to sit on his present one on the grounds that its height from the floor drew attention to the relative shortness of his legs .

48/94 Famous Graduate for Presenter: Sub-Committee Report

Dr Stormporch (best boy) spoke briefly on his sub-committee's report on the search for a well-known graduate of the university who might act as presenter of the university video. His sub-committee had recognised that what was required was a figure of similar appeal and status to Jonathan Miller or Melvin Bragg. Unfortunately, there were few equivalent graduates from this university. In the circumstances the sub-committee felt that the most suitable choice from past graduates was a Mr Russell Grant, the television expert on stars. The Chairman thanked Dr Stormporch for his report and asked if Mr Grant's area of televisual specialism was roughly that covered by Mr Patrick Moore. Dr Stormporch explained that Mr Grant's emphasis lay somewhat more on the predictive side of things. After a short debate it was agreed that Mr Grant be approached by the committee.

49/94 Any Other Business

Professor Stanstead (gaffer) reminded the committee that immediately after the next meeting on 5 April there would be a special showing of the award-winning feature film *Abbot and Costello Meet the Three Stooges*.

72 Ageing academics

Pressure is mounting for the Government to act on the ageing academic problem facing universities – THES

Dear Sir,
I don't want to complain but quite frankly in the past few years I've been finding it an increasing strain to carry student essays to and from my department. Can you help?

Yes indeed. We find that the Essay Trolley – see below – is a great help to all those who suffer from what experts now call Assessment Overweighting. As you can see, it is neatly compartmentalized for ease of reference, and is fitted with a brake capable of bringing it to a complete halt, even when moving downhill and laden with the equivalent of 12 Master's dissertations. Only £59.99.

Dear Sir,
I'm sorry to bother you with a trivial problem but I've recently begun to find that pointing to students for comments during the course of a seminar is producing severe pains in the upper arm. What do you recommend?

This is a problem which has only fully emerged in the past few years. Some elderly dons have resolved it by ignoring their students altogether and conducting the entire seminar themselves in a low monotone (to avoid voice strain). You may, however, prefer, to invest in the *Let's Hear From You Pointer*. A small key pad on the desk allows you to depress a button so as to swing the electronic hand round to the designated member of the group. £134.99.

Dear Sir,
I keep finding myself falling fast asleep at key departmental meetings. What do you recommend?

There is still a school of thought which favours the matchstick wedged beneath the eyelids but modern medical opinion tends to prefer the Automatic Leg Tingler. This tiny electronic device fits conveniently above the sock and is programmed to deliver a small electric shock whenever activated by any of the following phrases.

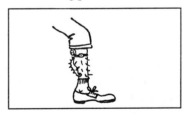

Surely, we should define our terms.
There seems to be some confusion here.
Perhaps we could have a comment from the student representatives.
Any other unstarred business?
Once again it looks as though the people at the far end of the table have had more than their fair share of the chocolate biscuits.

Only £49.99 (batteries not included).

73 Degree classifications

'There is an enormous amount of arbitrariness about (degree) classifications'
– Gareth Williams, Director of The Centre for Higher Education Studies at London University

Before we move on, Professor Lapping, might we look again at Candidate 307.

I thought we'd agreed a clear lower second.

Indeed. But I can't help but notice that we've just awarded an upper second to Candidate 487 even though that candidate's overall average on the 10 final papers was 58.37 whereas the overall average for Candidate 307 is 59.15.

But we applied Rule 6(a) to Candidate 487 and awarded an upper second on the grounds that their fourth down mark was 60. Candidate 307 has a fourth down mark of only 59.22.

Exactly my point. If you take the advantage which Candidate 307 enjoys over Candidate 487 on the overall average – a difference 0.78 – and add that to their fourth down mark of 59.22 you get a nice round 60 and therefore a clear upper second.

You can't do that.

Mr Odgers?

You can't take part of an overall average mark and use it to supplement one of the scores which makes up the average. That's contrary to Rule 12(a) which stresses the inviolability of average scores 'except in the case of Rounding Up when the average is less than 0.5 below the next degree class'.

Unless one invokes Rule 14(b) which says that 'in Special Cases the above rules may be suspended by the agreement of the Examining Board'.

But that's ruled out in this case by Rule 24(c) which insists that 'cases may not be labelled 'special' merely in order to query the degree class arising from the application of all other rules'.

This seems something of an impasse. I wonder if it would help our discussion if I revealed that Candidate 307 is Wagstaff.

Wagstaff!

Wagstaff!!

I'm surprised he found his way to the examination hall.

So it's a Lower Second for Candidate 307? Agreed.

Agreed.

Most satisfying. Yet another example of how strict application of our exam rules invariably produces the right answer.

74 Creative writing courses

'Creative writing will have to become a big part of university degree courses' – THES

Q.4. Which aspect of Western European culture was regarded by Max Weber as of critical importance in the emergence of capitalism?

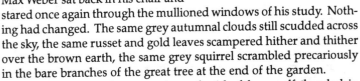

Max Weber sat back in his chair and stared once again through the mullioned windows of his study. Nothing had changed. The same grey autumnal clouds still scudded across the sky, the same russet and gold leaves scampered hither and thither over the brown earth, the same grey squirrel scrambled precariously in the bare branches of the great tree at the end of the garden.

It was all, he reflected, as unvarying as the tick of the grandfather clock in the corner of the room, as constant and repetitive as the sight of the paper which lay in front of him, that almost blank sheet of paper which provided the silent reminder that for six weeks now he had moved not one inch nearer to finding a solution to the problem which had come to bedevil his theoretical life.

What obsessed Max on this September day was not the richness of the harvest now being gathered in the fields beyond his garden, not the eternal cycle of seasons, but the emergence of one aspect of his material world to which even Nature herself could offer no solution. 'Why, oh why', he thought yet again to himself, allowing his eyes to roam around the scenes of accumulation outside the window – the bonfire of old leaves and branches, the towering golden haystacks in the distant meadows – 'Why, oh why, should capitalism have arisen in the west when it historically failed to appear in other countries which enjoyed similar technical and material opportunities?'

At that precise moment, Max felt a sudden stirring within himself. It was as though he had been taken over by an alien force, a force almost as powerful and insistent as the North wind which even now propelled another pile of autumn leaves in a reckless dance across the lawn. What was happening? He pinched himself. No, he was not dreaming. Perhaps then his mind was playing tricks. He glanced out of the window. Everything was normal.

But then, slowly, as though moved by an energy not his own, he picked up his pen, and underneath the question which had stayed there at the top of his paper for the last six weeks, under the question: 'Which aspect of Western European culture was regarded by Max Weber as of critical importance in the emergence of capitalism', he wrote in bold but faltering hand, *'The Protestant Ethic'*.

Outside the clouds seemed to slow momentarily; the grey squirrel paused in his labours, and even the golden leaves halted their merry dance. Only the ticking of the grandfather clock maintained its inexorable progress. Max leant back in his chair and smiled.

75 Quality II

Lord Joseph – formerly Sir Keith Joseph – told a conference at Wolfson College in Oxford that students and public deserved an academic equivalent of Which? to enable them to judge quality in higher education – The Independent

TEST RESULTS AND BEST BUYS FROM THREE STUDENT PROCESSING MACHINES

Twenty four students with a variety of personal and pedagogic problems (including deeply ingrained prejudices and severely tangled logic) were given eight hours' contact time with the following three models before being subjected to a re-test. The results were as follows:

The Lapping Semi-Automatic

Price. The exact cost of the Lapping and equivalent 'chairbound' models appears to vary from place to place but the average found by our researchers was £38,000.

Does it work? This conventional looking twin-seminar machine started well. There was a reassuring whirring noise as soon as it was switched on. However, testers reported that the efficiency of its operation soon became impeded by an extravagant amount of foam and froth. One or two nasty stains left over from A-level force feeding were eliminated, but after the eight hours several students appeared to have nasty rips in their self-confidence.

The Piercemüller Sabbatical

Price. On the face of it the Piercemüller Sabbatical at approximately £31,000 is considerably less expensive than the Lapping, but buyers should be aware of the warranty clause which requires it to be sent abroad every year for a three month extended service.

Does it work? The majority of our testers reported difficulties in actually starting up the Piercemüller. One or two were also disconcerted by the prominent red warning light bearing the legend: 'Half Loads Only', and by the machine's tendency to switch itself off half-way through a cycle and sit staring out of the nearest window.

The All Purpose Maureen

Price. Approximately £14,000.

Does it work? The Maureen took all the dirty student washing that could be thrown at it. It dealt readily and efficiently with tear-stains, severe stress, badly frayed egos, bruised identities, missing room numbers, lost theses, and deep existential angst.

Best Buy

If you're looking for a machine which will deal with all your pedagogic washday problems than there is none better than the All Purpose Maureen. Not only is this £17,000 cheaper than the nearest equivalent tenured model, but it occupies a third of the space, is slightly less likely to be discontinued, and while in operation does not emit the moaning sound which characterises other machines when they are required to deal with anything above the average workload.

Not Recommended

On the whole we feel unable to recommend the Piercemüller Sabbatical until such a time as it is fitted with a detectable on-off switch.

76 Student booklists

Student book-buying habits are to be investigated in a research project –
THES

Has everybody got a copy of the handout? Jolly good. Well, let's make a start. As usual, I'm going to spend the entire hour of this first seminar going very slowly through the book list. You'll notice that this particular list is six pages long, printed on A4 paper, and contains approximately 100 titles ...

Excuse me, Professor Lapping. But are all these books in the library?

Not *quite* all, Victoria. As you can see, some are marked N-I-L, which means NOT IN THE LIBRARY, some are marked O-M-F-L which means OFFICIALLY MISSING FROM THE LIBRARY.

But most have got another set of letters: L-S-I-T-B-I-S-B-N-E-C-F-I.

Quite true, Gerald. That stands for LIBRARY STAFF INSIST THIS BOOK'S IN STOCK BUT NO-ONE ELSE CAN FIND IT.

So how many on this list are actually in the library?

I can't say I've done an exact calculation, but there must be a good five per cent. You'll find most of the rest on sale in the campus book-shop. Yes, Rebecca?

But, Professor Lapping, there's about two pages of 'highly recommended'.

Then you must purchase the 'very highly recommended' texts indicated by a double asterisk. Yes, Anthony?

That's still too many to afford. There's over 20 'very highly'.

Then you have no option but to turn to the 'absolutely vital and utterly essential' category indicated by a treble asterisk. Yes, Jonathan?

I'm sorry, Professor Lapping, but which of the nine books with a treble asterisk would you say we really really need to buy?

You're asking for the most highly recommended book in the 'absolutely vital and utterly essential' list?

That's right.

Well, I suppose there's nothing quite so absolutely vital and utterly essential as the text by Lupin and Dogsbody. This one here. Yes, Alison?

Excuse me, Professor Lapping. But as that book is so absolutely vital and utterly essential for us all.

Yes, Alison.

D'you think we might borrow your copy until the end of term.

77 The research assessment exercise II

From the office of Professor Lapping

Dear Member of Staff,

The **HEFC Research Assessment Exercise** requires a complete list of all your publications in the period 1 January 1991 – 30 June 1994. Please send these to me by **midday tomorrow** categorised under the following headings.

1 **Books** written by yourself which are of absolutely no interest to anyone outside your own discipline. *1,500 points for each book (large, fat books, 500 points extra).*

2 **Books** written by yourself which might interest general readers. *5 points each.*

3 **Books** edited by you which contain six totally unrelated papers from a pointless academic conference. *1,000 points each.*

4 **Papers** given by you to high sounding conferences abroad while the other delegates were romping in the hotel swimming pool. *750 points each. (Deduct 100 points for Canadian conferences.)*

5 **Papers** written in the train and then delivered to bored colleagues in neighbouring academic institutions who were only there because of a three line whip from their head of department. *500 points per paper.*

6 **Articles** written for over-priced unread academic journals (minimum of two pages in length). *1,000 points each.*

7 **Articles** for popular journals. *2 points per dozen articles.*

8 **Reviews** of any academic book whatsoever irrespective of the length or quality of the review or of the book which prompted it. *300 points each review.*

9 **Paintings and sculpture** provided these are of academic subjects (a portrait of your Vice Chancellor is acceptable but not populist studies of sunflowers or people having lunch on the grass). *10 points each work.*

10 **Performance** e.g. stage portrayal of a relatively academic character ('Hamlet' but not 'Fortinbras'). *3 points each work.*

11 **Anything else of a strictly academic nature,** e.g. putting your course books in alphabetical order, painting university buildings, etc. *2 points each completed task.*

12 **Any old iron.** World-shattering creative work of a non-academic nature. *Forget it.*

Please note that several hundred sub-divisions of each of these categories are available on request from the HEFC Research Assessment Exercise. Mark your letters: *For the attention of the Mock Turtle.*

78 Marketing the department

Department of Media and Cultural Studies

Looking for an expert on media and cultural studies? Then look no further. All our top-ranking experts are trained in the art of media presentation (Dr Piercemüller has his own Camcorder, and Professor G. Lapping is a regular contributor to BBC Radio Poppleton's fortnightly discussion programme – *Mouthing Off*). All of them can offer the full range of contributions demanded by the modern media – from crisp 'soundbite' to a rambling inconclusive interview.

Choose your expert from:

Professor Gordon Lapping

As the author of such seminal monographs on cultural studies as *Pop icons or cultural iconoclasts?: Freddie and the Dreamers in context*, Professor Gordon Lapping has something interesting to say about most aspects of contemporary British culture including:

* Quite a few ways in which Budapest doesn't look at all like Paris in Gambon's *Maigret*.

 * A rather predictable argument about why *Thelma and Louise* wasn't really all that feminist.

Mr E. ("Ted") Odgers

Principal interests include the overthrow of contemporary corporate capitalism and bar billiards. Also available for comments on:

* What really happened at Kronstadt.

* Why I've still not been given a senior lectureship (extended monologue).

Maureen (Dept. Secretary)

Word processing, computing, student counselling, timetabling, filing, advanced accounting, all aspects of administration, student admissions, examination procedures, indexing, preparation of curriculum vitae, Xerox servicing, liaison with parents and external research bodies, conciliation and negotiation, first aid advice. Maureen is also able to offer:

* Modernism and Post-Modernism
* Advanced Hermeneutics and Phenomenology
* Beyond De-Constructionism.

Dr L. Piercemüller

As one of the leading authorities on contemporary linguistics Dr Piercemüller is ideally placed to make contributions to discussions on language (but preferably not anything to do with Chomsky). He is also able to offer:

* Short walks in the Tuscan countryside (particularly around Lucca).

* the quickest way to the Uffizi from the station.

Please note that all the above experts (except Maureen) have their own gown and will travel.

LIBRARY NEWS FOR SPRING TERM

Journal cancellation

The following journals have now been cancelled on the grounds that they were not constantly in use on every single day of last term:

The British Journal of Absolutely Essential Findings in Physics.

The European Journal of Vital Information in Modern Medicine.

The World Guide to Critical Current Developments in the Biological Sciences.

Opening Hours

We will be open this term from 11.45 am to 4.15 pm on Tuesdays, Wednesdays and Thursdays. No borrowings may take place after 4 pm, but as a result of an agreement with the Library Users group there will now be a 15 minute reading-up time for those already in possession of books.

Security

Security tags have now been fitted inside each book and may only be removed by the armed guard at the issue desk. (Please note that if you attempt to pass through the checkout with a tag still fitted an alarm will sound and you will be physically restrained by an overhead metallic arm).

Change of Name

As from the first day of term the *University Central Library (formerly the Gerald Ronson Central Library)* will again be re-named. From now on it will be known as the *University Information Centre* and the Chief Librarian will become the Director-General of Information Services. (It is hoped that these changes, apart from giving the Chief Librarian a new carpet, will also do something to deter visitors from asking: 'If this is the library, where are the books?'.)

Staff Changes

Ms Sarah Lofthouse, formerly with special responsibility for Evasive Answers at the Issue Counter is now in sole charge of Blaming the Computer at the Enquiries Desk.

Mr J.T.W. Harwhistle who has been responsible for Just Gone For Binding at the Issue Desk for the last 22 years has taken early retirement. Good luck to 'Stonewall' from all his colleagues.

Readings

Please note that as a further aid to students who find it difficult to obtain access to key texts, there will be readings at dictation speeds by junior librarians from the following essential works at 10.30 am on each opening day:

Tuesday   *Also Sprach Zarathüstra* Mrs Marion Fairweather

Wednesday   *The Origin of the Species* Ms Thelma Loomings

Thursday   *The Periodic Table of Elements* Mr Geoff Littlewood.

GIFTS FROM THE UNIVERSITY OF POPPLETON

Having problems with larger and larger seminar groups?...
This could be the answer

The University of Poppleton Loud Hailer
No more problems with hearing at the back
of the group thanks to this state-of-the-art
loud hailer. Use it constantly for all round
clarity or simply when introducing key
concepts.
£35 (batteries extra)

80 The student essay II

From the Departmental Secretary (Maureen)

Dear Third Year

As you will know the absolutely final ultimate deadline for submission of continuous assessment essays is Friday 21 May. These essays should observe the following (amended) departmental guidelines:

1 You are advised to type your essay (academic markers routinely save time by discriminating against students with 'childish' or 'difficult' handwriting).

2 Pay particular attention to your introduction and conclusion (they may be the only bits which ever get read).

3 Keep to the word limit (irrespective of your essay's length apologise for being 'slightly' over the word limit. This makes you seem conscientious while simultaneously obviating the need for the marker to make his/her own count).

4 Discuss outstanding problems with your course tutor before completing your final draft (pop in the day before the deadline and become downright hysterical about your inability to find two key references in the library).

5 Draw the threads of your argument together in your conclusion (or better still, make up a conclusive sounding quotation, e.g. 'There are no final words: only stuttered beginnings' – Nietzsche. 'There is a restless contingency about life which evades categorisation' – Emerson).

6 Additional marks are given for evidence of cross-cultural knowledge (scatter a few foreign phrases around, e.g. 'The Cultural Revolution *qua* revolution', or 'Dreams are, *pace* Freud, not always reminiscences', or 'There are no a *priori* reasons for assuming this to be the case'.

7 Make sure that your bibliography is complete (if you haven't read a vital book, cite it prominently in your bibliography).

8 Plagiarism is a serious and readily detectable offence (if you must copy, don't provide clues to your source by also quoting from the same text).

9 Examiners pay particular attention to analytical ability (use as many of the following terms as possible: syncretic, heuristic, teleological, epistemological, ontological, hegemonic, conjunctural).

10 Avoid expressions of personal opinion (never 'In my opinion', always 'According to recent commentators').

11 Use diagrammatic representation where appropriate (half-page shaded histograms have the edge on squiggly graphs).

12 Your final essay should resemble a published journal article (don't write THE END in block capitals at the end).

81 Exam results

Department of Media and Cultural Studies, Lapping speaking.

Oh, Professor Lapping, this is Louise Phelan. Third year. I'm sorry to bother you but I was ringing to see if the results were out yet.

Indeed they are, Louise. I have the list in front of me. Now let me see. Phelan. Phelan. Phelan ...

With a 'PH'.

Ah yes. Here we are. Well, it's time for congratulations, Louise.

It is?

Yes indeed. Many congratulations. You have an excellent lower second.

A lower second?

That's right. Well done. You can relax now. Got any holiday plans?

But I thought I would get an *upper* second. Dr Quintock said I would have no difficulty in getting an upper second.

One person's opinion isn't always ...

And Mr Odgers wrote on my tutorial report that I clearly had upper second potential. And you yourself wrote on my last essay, 'This is upper second work'.

You can't always generalise from a single piece of work ...

And in all my three years at Poppleton I've never had an essay mark below an upper second.

Y'know Louise, I think I'm beginning to sense the nature of our little problem. What you've been suffering from, Louise, is a little bit of over-confidence.

Over-confidence...

You'd over-confidently assumed that there'd be some necessary relationship between your own ability and our system of assessment. Am I right?

Well I ...

But don't worry about that now. Remember, you can always count on a good reference from this department. Now must rush. It seems to be my turn to take the external examiner to the station. Bye, Louise. And Louise.

Professor Lapping.

Good luck with the rest of your life.

Domestic Virtues

Sir, – I was extremely interested to read your report on the teaching of domestic science in colleges of higher education. As you say 'this is a subject area which has too frequently been regarded as of secondary academic importance because of its association with the banal household activities which constituted the subject in the schoolroom. It deserves better'.

Your readers may like to know that here at the South Melling College of Higher Education we take a very similar view. Not only do we select our students and staff in domestic science with extraordinary care, plan our courses with great conscientiousness and skill, but also do our utmost to maximise the employment prospects of our graduates. No wonder that our domestic science diploma was recently described by an external examiner as 'one of the best in the immediate region'!

Yours faithfully,
EDWARD BILLBOARD (Dr)
South Melling College of Higher Education

Name or Number

Sir, – We have been following with interest the recent discussion in your esteemed pages concerning the use of numbers rather than names on examination scripts. As you so lucidly say, 'although anonymity is hardly to be applauded as a characteristic of teacher – pupil interaction, there are occasions when the student's knowledge that their work will be graded entirely on its impersonal merits may be more a source of comfort than a matter of regret'.

Your readers may be interested to know that here at the Polytechnic of Hough Green we place great emphasis upon assessment procedures. All our students receive an enormous amount of individual attention from their exceptionally qualified tutors during the period of their courses, attention which ensures that they are more than adequately prepared for their final assessment. It is true that we still favour a 'names over numbers' approach but it is perhaps indicative of our success with this system that one external examiner recently described our finals papers as 'almost totally anonymous'.

Yours faithfully
GORDON HYPEMASTER
Deputy Principal The Polytechnic of Hough Green

Any Old Excuse

Sir, – It was with considerable relish that we read your recent editorial in which the words 'excellence' and 'quality' appeared.

Your readers may be fascinated to learn that here at the University of Poppleton we believe very strongly that the only way ahead is through a consistent emphasis on 'excellence' and 'quality' in all our courses, as well as in our competitively priced diploma courses for overseas students, and our luxurious en-suite conference facilities. Perhaps it was not for nothing that a recent independent report into universities in our part of the country concluded that 'Poppleton stands alone'.

Yours faithfully
CONSTANT PLUGGING
Vice Chancellor
University of Poppleton

83 Raising your research profile

!! HEADS OF DEPARTMENTS !!

* Do you have staff who contribute virtually nothing to your research publications?

* Are you anxious to free staff from onerous research tasks so they become available for vastly increased teaching loads?

* Does your department need a research boost to lift its rating?

* Are you one of the new university departments anticipating drastic cuts in your research component in the next selectivity exercise?

Then it's time to look at our brand new service

HIRE-A-DON CONTRACT RESEARCH

We have recently secured the EXCLUSIVE services of some of Britain's Top Research Dons. Although these dons are among the leading researchers in their fields they are currently operating on a freelance basis and therefore able to offer their services to YOU on attractive short-term contracts. Just look at some of the people who could be working for you:

Dr K.R. Lipchitz (Social Sciences) Dr Lipchitz (12 books and 124 articles) specialises in post-modernity and stratification. He is now available on an exclusive three-month contract during which he guarantees to produce at least FOUR articles for refereed journals. Total cost to your department: £25,000.

Professor P.B.W. Wainwright (Humanities) Professor Wainwright (14 books and 136 articles) specialises in 19th century European literature. He is at this very moment writing the last chapter of a major volume on *Literature and the Industrial Revolution*. Would you like him to be a member of YOUR department when he sends in that last chapter? Professor Wainwright could be yours for just £36,000 for a six-month contract.

Dr K.R. Tobler (Physics) Dr Tobler (five books and 974 articles) has just completed a major research project into the kinetics of gaseous reaction at very low temperatures. It is modestly estimated that this research will be written up in a minimum of 27 articles. Can't you just see them in YOUR next research submission? Dr Tobler is available on the following generous terms: £1,000 per week (ONE article guaranteed) or £5,000 per month (FIVE articles guaranteed).

* Top Research Dons require no accommodation or other university facilities.

* They need not even visit your department during their period of research incumbency.

* You simply sit back and let them do the research.

ACT NOW AND WATCH *YOUR* RESEARCH RANKING RISE

84 Citations

The British Journal of Citation Studies, Vol 14 No 84 February 1992.
Some comments on the Role of Academic Citations in the Calculation of Research Standing in Higher Education
By Dr D. B. W. Piercemüller (Department of Media and Cultural Studies, University of Poppleton).

In recent years (Brown, 1988; Letkin and Willsop, 1990) it has been suggested (Campbell and Pitbody, 1991) that we measure the relative research standing (Doomladen, 1984) of academics by counting up the number of citations their work has received in properly refereed journals (Pastmaster and Lackey, 1989). What I want to say in this present article (Piercemüller, 1992), is that I think there is a real danger that this might eventually lead to lots of articles like this (Piercemüller, 1992) which had almost nothing to say (Planchette and Titwillow, 1986) and did little more than provide an opportunity for academics to name drop unashamedly in order to ensure that their friends received a high citation count at the end of the year (Brown, 1988; Letkin and Willsop, 1990; Campbell and Pitbody, 1991; Doomladen, 1984; Pastmaster and Lackey, 1989; Planchette and Titwillow, 1986; and anybody else who knows me). That's my opinion anyway (Piercemüller, 1992).

References
Brown, D.J. (1988) 'What is recent?: Some problems with the notion of Chronological nearness', *British Journal of Opening Remarks in Journal Articles*, No 7 pps 34-35.
Campbell, J.C. and Pitbody, P.B. (1991) 'Suggestions, proposals, and intimations: Austin revisited', *The Western Australian Journal of Linguistic Hair-splitting*, No 37 pps 46-326.
Doomladen, W. (1984) *The Guinness Book of the Top One Thousand and One Academic Researchers*. Pergamon Press.
Letkin, B.R. and Willsop, K.L. (1990) 'How recent is recent?', *Journal for the De-construction of Journal Articles*, No 4 p 124.
Pastmaster, H.S. and Lackey, D.B. (1989) 'Choosing the Right Whistle', *British Journal of Contemporary Refereeing*, Vol 24 pps 17-56.
Piercemnller, D.B.W. (1992) *Ibid.*
Planchette, S.P. and Titwillow, K. (1986)'Articles Which Have absolutely Nothing to Say', *The Canadian Journal of Philosophical Advances*, Vol 88 pps 18-88.

This Week's Research Grants
Professor G. Lapping, University of Poppleton, twenty quid from the ESRC for nothing much at all except sheer endurance in the face of repeated and quite diverse rejections.

85 Finals

DEPARTMENT OF MEDIA AND CULTURAL STUDIES

From Your Departmental Secretary (Maureen)

Dear Member of Department

What with all the leaves on the trees and the longer evenings you might have guessed that we are once again moving nearer to the time of year we traditionally call Finals. This means that even now I should be preparing myself to perform the following modest duties:

1 Five days sitting around the office receiving continuous assessment essays, issuing receipts for same, and listing those which arrive after the final deadline.

2 One day counselling distraught students who failed to meet the final deadline.

3 Four days sorting hundreds of essays into course areas and dispatching them in large brown envelopes to appropriate marking partners.

4 Two days listening to slanderous complaints from individual members of staff about their marking partner.

5 Three days on the telephone to Dr Piercemüller debating the vagaries of the Italian postal system.

6 Four days finding a restaurant for the external examiner's dinner which simultaneously caters for heavy-rock carnivore smokers and folk-loving non-smoking vegans.

7 Three days packaging 'disputed scripts' into parcel for external examiner.

8 One day counselling External Examiner over the size of his parcel.

9 Two days eating biscuits at interminable examiners' meetings.

10 One day typing out degree results and dealing with telephone enquiries from students about individual grades.

11 Five days counselling lower-second and third-class graduands.

In the past, I have, of course, been only too delighted to carry out these 31 days of extra duties in addition to those normally associated with my post of departmental secretary. But this year I feel I have a migraine coming on. Not to mention some severe anxiety. And the old palpitation. And writer's block. And a bit of stress. And difficulties at home. And problems with the time of month.

Quite frankly, all in all, I'd like an aegrotat.

Yours sincerely,

Maureen (medical note on request)

THIS WEEK'S CONFERENCES

ACADEMIC FREEDOM AND INSTITUTIONAL AUTONOMY IN THE MIDDLE 1990s

A seemingly interminable one-day conference at which a senior minister makes a meandering speech totally failing to address any of the points raised in earlier sessions by well-meaning but impotent liberal academics.

Venue: A large country house somewhere near London.

Participation: By invitation only – but quite frankly numbers are usually so low they're glad to take anyone at the last minute.

ANNUAL MEETING OF THE BRITISH ASSOCIATION FOR VERY EXPERIMENTAL ANIMAL PSYCHOLOGY

Papers to be given:

Differential Recall of Nonsense Syllables by Partially Lobotomized Pigeons.

Patterns of Underwater T-Maze Learning in the Male Octopus.

Methodological Problems in the Inducement of Cocaine 'Snorting' in the Laboratory Rat.

Venue: Up on the roof of a psychology building somewhere near you.

Participation: Confined to sinister looking men with rimless glasses and deficient social skills.

NATIONAL ASSOCIATION OF UNIVERSITY REGISTRARS

A four-day conference at which the following papers will be given:

Improving the Vice Chancellor's Image: The Case for Skin Grafts.

Passing the Buck to the Bursar.

Venue: Gritti Palace Hotel, Venice.

Participation: Registrars only (sorry, no women).

WHO WILL APPRAISE THE APPRAISERS?

A two day colloquium at which academic appraisees and their academic appraisers appraise the recently introduced academic appraisal system.

Venue: The Vivaldi Room, University of Loughborough.

Participation: Open to all appraisers and appraisees (subject to appraisal).

WHITHER BISCUITS? (sponsored by United Biscuits Plc)

A five-day conference on the future of biscuits in the UK. Topics and speakers include:

Biscuits: I love them (Professor G. Lapping).

Biscuits in Mediterranean Climes – with slides (Dr L. Piercemüller).

Venue: The Ginger Snap Lecture Theatre, University of Buckingham.

Participation: All those anxious for whatever reason to ingratiate themselves with United Biscuits.

(That's enough conferences – *ed.*)

APPOINTMENTS
UNIVERSITY OF
POPPLETON

TOKEN MAN

Applications are invited from
suitably qualified *persons* for the
above post in the university's
distinguished department of
gender studies. The position
becomes vacant as a result of a
recent decision by the Universities
Ethics Committee that whilst it
was in philosophical agreement
with the claims by the gender
studies department that there
were good epistemological
reasons for currently confining the
teaching of gender studies to
women only, this did appear on
the face of it to constitute an *a priori*
breach of equal
opportunities legislation.
No teaching or research duties
are currently attached to the
post but the successful candidate will be required to fulfil
such ceremonial functions as
posing for departmental and
degree day group photo-
graphs, signing themselves as
'Mr' in letters to THES from
the department, and occasion-
ally serving as a silent exhibit in
the popular second-year
undergraduate course on 'The
Myth of Penis Envy'.
(Since, as we've said, there are
no other men in the department, applications from men
for this position would be
particularly welcomed.)

87 Student tracking

A new software package will help universities maintain comprehensive records of students' personal and academic career at university – The Times

Name — Lucy Parsons

Age on completion of course — 20.8 years

Course — B.A. Cultural and Media Studies

Principal Supervisor — Dr Piercemüller (in absentia)

Completed Modules (short title)

Top of the Pops (2 modules)
Early Hitchcock (1 module)
Late Derrida (un-moduled)
Coronation St. (4 modules)
Raymond Williams (half module)
Reading Madonna (4 modules)
Walter Benjamin (1 module)
Analysing Batman (2 modules)
Understanding Modules
(3 modules)

Accommodation Address(es) during course:

Year One — Shared room – B Wing, Winnie Mandela Hall

Year Two — Shared flat in Poppleton with three other students, an unemployed personal growth therapist, and a lot of empty milk bottles

Year Three — Shared Room – B wing, Winnie Mandela Hall

Financial Status — All fees and library fines paid. Outstanding student loan – £4,568.22

Health Record

Year One: — Visited University Medical Centre to complain about severe headaches
Diagnosis: Exam nerves
Prescription: Panadol

Year Two: — Visited University Medical Centre to complain about malnutrition
Diagnosis: Exam nerves
Prescription: Panadol

Year Three: — Visited University Medical Centre to talk about her total lack of interest in the course and life in general
Diagnosis: Exam nerves
Prescription: Panadol

University Societies

Year One: — Revolutionary Communist Party

Year Two: — Star Trek Appreciation Club

Year Three: — Ballroom Dancing Society

General Summary of Student by Head of Department

Lucy Parsons is a difficult student to assess in that she did not bring herself to the attention of any of her tutors. She was in many ways a type of student who went her own way and did, as it were, her own thing. So, overall, to sum up, I would say with considerable confidence that she was very much a student who was, without any doubt at all, at this university and, what is more, in this precise department.

G. Lapping (Professor and H.O.D).

CONFIDENTIAL COMPUTER PASSWORD – LUCY PARSONS

88 Summer teaching

Who's there?

Woof, woof.

Behind the photocopier.

Woof, woof.

Dr Piercemüller why are you barking like that? And on all fours.

Ah, Maureen, there you are. Didn't want to disturb anyone. Only here for a second. Got to pop over to the garden centre and then try and beat the rush hour.

Dr Piercemüller, did you get my last note?

Which note was that, Maureen?

My last note. About your summer arrangements.

Oh yes. My summer arrangements. Nice of you to ask. Very thoughtful. Yes, roughly speaking, I'll be in the Var.

The Var?

That's right. We'll fly over to Nice and then straight up to the hills with maybe a lunch stop in Vence.

Vence?

You thought I was going to say St Paul de Vence, didn't you? But that's very much a tourist trap these days. And then on to a villa near Draguignan for a few weeks and then when August is over and the tourists have gone we'll be down to our little place in Antibes. Only a stone's throw from where old Graham Greene used to hang out. Oh yes, it's amazing what you can pack into a couple of months. Anything else you need to know?

One small thing.

Yes.

When exactly will you be packing in your five weeks intensive summer teaching on the brand new two-year Cultural Studies degree?

There's teaching during the summer? During the actual summer vacation? D'you know, Maureen, I think it might be wise to have some sort of back-up for me. Obviously, I'd love to participate but I do anticipate some delay in getting back into the country. It could be as long as two months.

A two month delay?

Quarantine regulations, Maureen.

Woof, woof, Dr Piercemüller.

Woof, woof, Maureen.

89 The HEFC I

HEFC will audit research returns where 'discrepancies are identified'

Professor Gordon Lapping
Department of Media and Cultural Studies
University of Poppleton

Dear Professor Lapping,

We are in receipt of Form RA2a relating to your department together with appropriate entries in the 12 principal categories and the 8 sub-categories of Section 12.

Thank you for returning this form so promptly and for placing the lading documents in an envelope marked 'Lading Documents' (as requested in our letter of 26 May – *Section 12: Lading Documents*).

As you will be aware the Council has expressed concern that there might be certain 'discrepancies' on RA2as and I am now writing to say that the following 'discrepancies' have been detected on your own forms. We would welcome your comments on these so that we may decide whether or not to move to a 'detailed audit' of your department's research work.

The "discrepancies" are as follows:

1   Dr Piercemüller of your department is given as the author of a book (*The Origin of the Species*) which you have asterisked as 'of major significance in the field'. Whilst Council felt it entirely appropriate to asterisk this task, further evidence was required that it was solely the work of the stated author.

2   Under the headings 'Patents' there is a reference to a departmental member described as 'Maureen', and the number 192512/45/871/ BD/44. Some concern was expressed that there might have been a transcription error. According to the Patent Office, this number refers to the invention of the internal combustion engine.

3   Under the heading 'major academic distinctions' you describe Dr Quintock as having successfully acquired the 'NBRC'. Our preliminary enquiries suggest that this may not be a sufficiently conventional mark of academic distinction in that the letters record membership of the National Breakdown Recovery Club.

4   Council was pleased to note the wide-ranging interests of your department but there was a technical reservation about your own entry under 'original contributions to music'. Would you please confirm that your work – *Der Ring des Nibelungen* – was completed since the RA2a qualifying date of January 1992?

Yours sincerely

D.W. Mock-Turtle
(Principal RA2a Assessment Officer)

90 Quality III

Ah, Dr Piercemüller. Professor Lapping will see you now.

Thank you, Maureen.

Piercemüller.There you are. Do come in. Sorry to bother you on your research term but I wanted to make certain you were fully up to date with the next departmental phase of TQM.

TQM?

Total Quality Management.

What else?

As you'll remember we installed precise TQM targets last term in critical areas of departmental performance and set ourselves the goal of achieving these by the application of the principle of creating constancy of purpose for improvement of product and service.

It all comes flooding back.

Always remembering of course that a pre-condition for advancement in TQM is that we successfully diagnose the variations in the system and decide which are due to variations in human abilities and which are caused by the system.

What other pre-condition for advancement could there be?

Exactly. We have to be aware, Dr Piercemüller, that the only way to survive is through learning how better to manage resources. That's our job, learning how to manage the right way, learning how to manage for Quality.

Learning how to manage for Quality.

That's absolutely right. We can only move ahead by successful problem identification, data gathering, data analysis and the generation of proposals for solution, implementation and test.

The generation of proposals for solutions, implementation and test.

Precisely. Well, thank you, Dr Piercemüller. You've obviously taken to heart the essential lesson that those who would teach quality to others should be examples of what they would like to see done in the name of quality.

That in my view is the essential lesson.

It is after all only by insisting on Quality and continuously improving Quality that we can achieve true Quality in every area of Quality and continue the cycle of the never-ending improvement of Quality. That couldn't be clearer could it, Dr Piercemüller?

Only if you removed that waste paper basket from your head and put down the bunch of flowers.

Thank you, Dr Piercemüller. That's all for today. Onwards to profound knowledge.

Ever onwards, Professor Lapping.

91 Staff behaviour in the departmental office

From: Professor Lapping

To: All Members of Staff

Subject: Staff Behaviour in the Departmental Office

I do hope that you had a good holiday and have returned with your batteries recharged.

You will be pleased to hear that I have now completed the analysis of data from the video camera installed in the Departmental Office under our Total Quality Scheme. The findings are as follows:

1 **Excessive wandering:** 4.2 members of staff were regularly observed coming into the departmental office for a general wander. The typical pattern involved a careful perusal of old posters, an extended look over Maureen's shoulder, a chat with anyone who happened to be around, a few moments staring out the window at some distant object, and then a slow exit. Average time wasted was 12.2 minutes per wander. Total number of wanders: 427.

2 **The Piercemüller Pop-In:** Visible only in slow motion analysis. The door is partially opened and a face appears for no more than 0.5 of a second during which the following cry is emitted. 'Everything all right, Maureen?' then the door closes. The visit is subsequently cited as proof that the member of staff was available for discussion with students. Total number of observed instances: 1.

3 **Is there something wrong?** This office phrase, which was uttered to the accompaniment of some banging and shouting, took different forms:

   (a) Is there something wrong with this word processor?

   (b) Is there something wrong with this stapler?

   (c) Is there something wrong with this list of first years?

Such questions were repeated until Maureen completed the task in hand. Total recorded instances: 312.

4 **Constant postal checks**: Although there have been just two postal deliveries a day since the foundation of this university, several members of staff were observed approaching their postal pigeonholes at frequent intervals between deliveries. Average no. of visits to pigeonhole between deliveries: 6.8. Average time between inspection of pigeonhole: 27 minutes.

5 **No mail today:** A variation on the above problem is the persistent tendency of members of staff who rarely receive any mail to ask Maureen 'if the mail has come up yet'. Average number of such questions to Maureen during a typical day: 14.6.

I trust you will take these observations on board and proceed, where appropriate, to modify your own behaviour.

92 The HEFC II

Remember our slogan *'Never mind the sodding depth, count the bleeding Quality'.*

Enjoying the pudding, Roger?

Yes, thank you, Mother. Very rich.

Not too much candied peel?

No, just right.

And how are things at 'the university'? Is your department still doing well?

We're a '2'. Our department's a '2'. In the research ratings.

That's very good. I'm sure if you all work hard you could be a '1' next year. More port wine sauce? I made it with seville oranges. Just as Delia says.

You don't understand, Mother, '1' is worse than '2'. We have to try to become '3'. And then a '4'.

Really?

And we're only 'satisfactory' at teaching. We thought we were excellent. That's what we told the HEFC. But they wrote back and said 'Oh no you're not. You're only satisfactory'.

But otherwise it's going well.

No, it's not. In fact, it's going very badly indeed. I get these constant headaches because of all the teaching I have to do. And the carpet in my room is now so thin that the rubber underlay is showing through. And we can't make phone calls in the morning.

Roger. It is Christmas. Do try and jolly up a little.

And there are all these people who used to work in polytechnics walking around calling themselves 'dons' and there's even one new Vice Chancellor with a ring stuck through his ear.

You mustn't let them upset you.

And where there used to be an academic community, a set of shared intellectual and pedagogic values, there's now nothing but a selfish, individual, alienated concern with how one rates on some absurd index of personal or departmental quality.

But life's not all that bad, darling.

Mother, how can you say that?

Look down at your plate.

What?

You've got the silver sixpence.

Crikey, so I have. Happy Christmas, Mother.

130

93 New Year's resolutions

As usual we invite a number of distinguished people from the world of higher education to describe their hopes, wishes, and resolutions for the New Year.

The Vice Chancellor of the University of Poppleton

1994 will undoubtedly be a time for new opportunities. At the forefront of our thinking will be a determined effort to sustain our exciting new programme of student cutbacks. With courage and good sense it should be possible in the coming year to exclude significantly large numbers of perfectly well qualified students. Together we can win. Thank you.

The editor of The THES

There is a generally accepted view, in the sense that any single view can be said to be generally accepted, that this is an appropriate time of the year for making what are commonly known as 'resolutions'. In recent years, there have been those who have raised doubts about this annual festival of good intentions. In particular, there have been questions about the proportion of such resolutions which are, in the language of this debate, 'kept'. But surely this is to miss, or at least partly to miss, the point. What we have to bear in mind is the necessity of completing at least another three columns of this discussion and then producing a final paragraph which sounds at least vaguely prescriptive. Without doing this, we will leave ourselves very much where we started at the beginning. We will, and let there be no doubt about it, be left without a new year editorial.

Maureen (department secretary)

I didn't really expect to be here. But now that I am I wonder if I might take this opportunity to remind all members of the cultural and media studies department of the urgent need to complete their tutorial reports and have them back at the very latest by 5 Jan. This means you!

John Patten

I'd like to send New Year greetings to all readers of *The THES*. On second thoughts I don't want to have anything to do with the readers of *The THES*. What I really want to know is this: if universities are so proud of themselves then why do so few of them fly their maces from the top of the administrative block? And I had another good idea about higher education a moment ago. But I seem to have forgotten it.

Dave Spandling (Senior Quality Officer with the HEQC and member of the higher education quality working party on higher quality)

My simple resolution is to keep saying 'quality' on every possible occasion. It won't make a scrap of difference to anything whatsoever but look where it's got me.